THE COZY CHRISTMAS MOVIE COOKBOOK

Mouthwatering Food to Enjoy During Your Favorite Holiday Films

Holly Carpenter

Skyhorse Publishing

Copyright © 2020 by Hollan Publishing

Skyhorse Publishing books may be purchased in bulk at special discounts for sales promotion, corporate gifts, fund-raising, or educational purposes. Special editions can also be created to specifications. For details, contact the Special Sales Department, Skyhorse Publishing, 307 West 36th Street, 11th Floor, New York, NY 10018 or info@skyhorsepublishing.com.

Skyhorse® and Skyhorse Publishing® are registered trademarks of Skyhorse Publishing, Inc.®, a Delaware corporation.

Visit our website at www.skyhorsepublishing.com.

10 9 8 7 6 5 4 3 2 1

Library of Congress Cataloging-in-Publication Data is available on file.

Design by Joanna Williams
Images used under license by Shutterstock.com

Print ISBN: 978-1-5107-5957-2
Ebook ISBN: 978-1-5107-5950-3

Printed in China

DISCARD

CONTENTS

INTRODUCTION

Every little detail of a Christmas movie is designed to give viewers the perfect holiday, from the decorations in the background to the festive clothing on the characters. And no perfect Christmas would be complete without all of your favorite holiday treats! Those crafty filmmakers fill frames with beautifully decorated cookies, elaborate Christmas feasts, and hundreds of cups of hot cocoa to make your mouth water for Christmas.

Does watching Lacey Chabert whip up gingerbread creations in *The Sweetest Christmas* make you want to bake? Do you start to crave Luke Bennett's signature Turkey Pot Pie, or find yourself searching for the traditional dishes Karla serves at Snow Valley Lodge? Well, you must have been very good this year, because Santa granted your secret wish—a companion cookbook just for you!

The Cozy Christmas Movie Cookbook brings you 100 recipes inspired by dozens of your favorite films and their loveable characters. You'll find everything from cocoa to cocktails, party snacks to elaborate mains, and all of the sweet treats you can handle. And every recipe will fill you with the Christmas spirit and memories of your favorite movie moments. Much like the *Countdown to Christmas*, there's something for everyone in *The Cozy Christmas Movie Cookbook*! So, cozy up on the couch with a warm beverage and get ready for the most wonderful time of the year!

CHAPTER 1:

MOVIE NIGHT IN

CLEM'S NORTHPOLE SNOWY COCOA

Serves 4

Enjoy while watching *Northpole*

2014 — Starring Tiffani Thiessen as Chelsea Hastings, Josh Hopkins as Ryan Wilson, and Bailee Madison as Clementine

Ordinary hot cocoa deserves a magical makeover at Christmastime, and who better to help with that than Santa's own elves? Clem's Snowy Cocoa combines white chocolate with peppermint for a perfectly jolly pick-me-up after a long sleighride south.

4	cups favorite milk
8	ounces white chocolate, chopped
1	teaspoon pure vanilla extract
½	teaspoon peppermint extract
	Whipped cream, for serving
	Candy cane or crushed peppermints, for serving

1. Combine the milk and white chocolate in a medium saucepan over medium-low heat. Stir occasionally until the white chocolate has melted and the mixture comes to a slight simmer. Remove the pan from the heat.

2. Stir in the vanilla and peppermint extracts, then divide the cocoa into individual mugs or heat-safe drinking glasses.

3. Top each with whipped cream and garnish with a candy cane or a dusting of crushed peppermint (or both!).

HOMESTEAD'S OWN COOKIE-INSPIRED COCOA

Serves 2

Enjoy while watching *Christmas in Homestead*

2016 — Starring Taylor Cole as Jessica McEllis and Michael Rady as Matt Larson, plus Katrina Norman as Zoe Larson

Christmas is a time to come together, and nothing says "peace offering" like a cup of cocoa that tastes like a snickerdoodle cookie. As an entrepreneurial future owner of a chain of charming small-town inns, Zoe Larson would offer nothing less than her signature drink to shivering paparazzo Zac. Top each liquid olive branch with whipped cream and a sprinkling of ground cinnamon.

3	cups favorite milk, divided
⅔	cup chopped white chocolate
1	cinnamon stick
½	teaspoon pure vanilla extract
½	teaspoon ground cinnamon
⅛	teaspoon ground nutmeg
	Whipped cream, for serving
	Cinnamon, for serving

1. Add ¼ cup of the milk, all of the white chocolate, and the cinnamon stick to a medium saucepan over low heat. Stir until the white chocolate melts completely.

2. Stir in the remaining milk, vanilla, cinnamon, and nutmeg until the mixture is combined and heated through.

3. Remove the cinnamon stick and pour the cocoa into heat-safe glasses to serve.

GIVE ME S'MORE HOT CHOCOLATE

Serves 2

Enjoy while watching **Christmas Getaway**

2017 — Starring Bridget Regan as Emory Blake and Travis Van Winkle as Scott Hays,
plus Raven Stewart as Katy Hays

As travel writer Emory Blake discovers, gathering around an open fire to toast marshmallows is just one wonderful part of a log-cabin Christmas. Every sip of this cocoa is like experiencing the magic of a s'more for the very first time. And with just two servings, it's the perfect excuse to cozy up to that ruggedly handsome single dad you just met!

3	cups favorite milk
¼	cup cocoa powder
2	tablespoons chocolate syrup
3	tablespoons granulated sugar
1	pinch kosher salt
	Extra chocolate syrup, for serving
	Graham crackers, crushed for serving
4	marshmallows, for serving
2	drink skewers, for serving (optional)

"A person who believes in Santa is a fundamentally good person. It means they believe in hope."

—Ashley Harrison, *Dashing through the Snow*

1. Warm the milk in a medium saucepan over medium heat for about 5 minutes, being careful not to overheat it.

2. Whisk in the cocoa powder, chocolate syrup, sugar, and salt until thoroughly combined and warmed, then remove the pan from the heat.

3. Prepare your mugs by lightly dipping the rims in chocolate syrup and then in the crushed graham crackers. Divide the hot chocolate into the prepared mugs.

4. Toast your marshmallows in a toaster oven, a regular oven, over a flame, or using a culinary blow-torch before placing two in each mug, threading skewers through them if you like.

Note: You could place oven-safe mugs with untoasted marshmallows on a baking sheet under the oven broiler for a few seconds, being especially careful not to burn yourself when you remove them.

5. Top with an extra drizzle of chocolate syrup and a dusting of graham cracker before serving.

A CORDINIAN CHRISTMAS MIRACLE

Serves 4
Enjoy while watching A Royal Christmas
2014 – Starring Lacey Chabert as Emily Taylor and Stephen Hagan as Prince Leopold

This creamy, white hot chocolate is like a snowy white Christmas (or a "Cordinian Christmas Miracle") and a warm blanket combined in a cup. For a royal touch, serve it in your fanciest heat-safe glasses and drink it with head and pinky finger held high.

4	cups favorite milk
1	teaspoon pure vanilla extract
1	cup white chocolate chips
	Whipped cream or marshmallows, for serving

1. In a medium saucepan, stir together the milk, vanilla, and white chocolate over medium-low heat until the chocolate melts and the mixture begins to simmer.

2. Immediately divide the mixture into mugs, top with whipped cream or marshmallows (or both), and enjoy while hot.

SALTED CARAMEL HOT CHOCOLATE

Serves 2

Enjoy while watching *Matchmaker Santa*

2012 – Starring Lacey Chabert as Melanie Hogan and Adam Mayfield as Dean Ford

No self-respecting baker would serve up boring hot chocolate when they could whip up a confection-inspired treat instead. Luckily, this indulgent cocoa is simple enough for even Peggy and Debbie to follow. Top it off with a big dollop of whipped cream drizzled with caramel to create a cup fit for a bakery window.

2   cups favorite milk

½   cup bittersweet chocolate chips

½   cup salted caramel sauce

      Whipped cream, for serving

      Extra caramel sauce, for serving

1. Warm the milk in a small saucepan over medium heat for about 5 minutes, being careful not to overheat it.

2. Whisk in the chocolate chips and caramel sauce until melted and combined.

3. Remove the pan from the heat and allow the cocoa to cool slightly before dividing. Serve topped with whipped cream and caramel sauce.

BARB'S FAMOUS HOT CHOCOLATE

Serves 4

Enjoy while watching *A Wish for Christmas*

2016 – Starring Lacey Chabert as Sara Thomas and Paul Greene as Peter Williams, plus Colleen Wheeler as Barb Williams

A cup of this delicious hot chocolate is enough to make an estranged son come home for Christmas—with or without important business in the area. While Peter's mom, Barb, prefers to garnish her hot chocolate with an intricately decorated marshmallow snowman, a candy cane will do.

3	cups favorite milk
¼	cup granulated sugar
2	tablespoons cocoa powder
1	cup semisweet chocolate chips
1	teaspoon pure vanilla extract
	Whipped cream, for serving

1. Add the milk to a small saucepan and bring it to a simmer over medium heat. Whisk in the sugar and cocoa powder until smooth.

2. Stir in the chocolate chips and vanilla extract until melted and well combined, then remove the mixture from the heat.

3. Divide the cocoa into mugs, top each cup with whipped cream, and enjoy while hot.

IRISH COFFEE

— Serves 1 —

Enjoy while watching your favorite Christmas movie

Just like a cozy Christmas movie, this spirited coffee-based beverage will warm you from the inside out. The important thing is to use Folger's coffee. As you binge-watch the Countdown to Christmas, keep an eye out for that ever-present red canister or tub.

1 cup hot brewed Folger's coffee

1 tablespoon Irish cream liqueur

Irish whiskey, to taste

1 teaspoon light brown sugar (optional)

Thick whipped cream, for serving

Chocolate shavings (optional)

1. Combine the coffee, Irish cream liqueur, and whiskey in a mug or heat-safe glass.

2. Add up to 1 teaspoon of the brown sugar, if you like your drinks extra sweet.

3. Finish with as much whipped cream as you like before serving. Top it off with chocolate shavings for an even more decadent drink.

RED CARPET COCOA

Serves 4

Enjoy while watching ***Christmas in Homestead***

2016 – Starring Taylor Cole as Jessica McEllis and Michael Rady as Matt Larson

Major movie star Jessica McEllis is used to having the red carpet rolled out for her, even in small-town bakeries. This red velvet cocoa, inspired by one of her favorite treats, would surely live up to her Hollywood standards—even if it's made in Iowa. Cream cheese whipped cream is the perfect icing on this sweet treat.

Cream Cheese Whipped Cream

¼   cup heavy cream

4   ounces cream cheese, softened

½   cup granulated sugar

1   pinch kosher salt

½   teaspoon pure vanilla extract

Red Velvet Cocoa

4   cups favorite milk

¼   cup granulated sugar

1   (10-ounce) package mini semisweet chocolate chips

2   teaspoons red food coloring

1   teaspoon pure vanilla extract

For the whipped cream:

1. Add the cream to a large bowl. Use a hand mixer, starting on low and gradually increasing the speed, to whip it until soft peaks form, about 5–10 minutes.

2. In a second large bowl, use the hand mixer to combine the cream cheese, sugar, salt, and vanilla until creamy. Fold in the whipped cream until well combined and fluffy.

3. Refrigerate the whipped cream until the hot chocolate is ready to serve.

"Christmas is like a baton, passed down from one generation to the next. It reminds us of who we are and where we came from."

—Karla Lewis, *Let It Snow*

For the hot chocolate:

1. Add the milk and sugar to a medium saucepan, bring the mixture to a simmer over medium heat, and stir until the sugar dissolves.

2. Remove the pan from the heat and whisk in the chocolate chips until melted and combined.

3. Whisk in the food coloring and vanilla, then divide the mixture into 4 mugs. Top each with a dollop of your prepared whipped cream.

WORLD-FAMOUS LONG FAMILY EGGNOG

―――――― **Serves 6** ――――――

*Enjoy while watching **Finding Santa***

2017 – Starring Eric Winter as Ben White and Jodie Sweetin as Grace Long

It's not a Christmas movie if it doesn't feature at least one cup of eggnog. If you can't get enough of this creamy drink, take a page from Grace's book and whip up this mixture for breakfast. For a little extra warmth on a winter evening, simply add a cup of light rum to the mixture before refrigerating it.

2	cups whole milk
3	whole cloves
2	pods star anise
1	teaspoon pure vanilla extract
1	teaspoon ground cinnamon
¾	teaspoon ground nutmeg
1	pinch kosher salt
6	large egg yolks
¾	cup granulated sugar
2	cups half-and-half
2	tablespoons pure vanilla extract
1	cup heavy cream
	Extra ground nutmeg, for serving

1. Combine the milk, cloves, star anise, 1 teaspoon vanilla, cinnamon, nutmeg, and salt in a large saucepan over medium-low heat. Allow the mixture to warm for 5 minutes, then turn up the heat to just below medium-high and stir until the mixture comes to a boil. Immediately remove it from the heat and set it aside.

2. Whisk together the egg yolks and sugar in a large bowl until combined and fluffy. Slowly and carefully pour the hot mixture into the egg mixture a bit at a time, whisking briskly as you go.

3. Pour the combined mixture into the saucepan and cook over medium heat, stirring constantly, until the eggnog is thick and fluffy, about 5 minutes. (Don't let the liquid boil.)

4. Strain the eggnog to remove the cloves and star anise and let the eggnog cool. Stir in the half-and-half and 2 tablespoons of vanilla, then refrigerate the mixture overnight.

5. The next day, whip the heavy cream until fluffy, then fold it into the eggnog. Divide the finished mixture into glasses and top it off with a dusting of nutmeg before serving.

IT'S-NOT-CHRISTMAS-WITHOUT GINGERBREAD EGGNOG

———— *Serves 4* ————

Enjoy while watching Once Upon a Christmas Miracle

2018 – Starring Brett Dalton as Chris Dempsey and Aimee Teegarden as Heather Krueger

Liver donor Chris and lucky recipient Heather are proof that eggnog and Christmas cookies are a powerful combination. This twist on the traditional holiday drink combines that recipe for love into one cup.

———

6	large egg yolks
½	cup granulated sugar
2	cups whole milk
1	cinnamon stick
¼	teaspoon pure vanilla extract
1	pinch kosher salt
1	teaspoon freshly grated nutmeg
¼	teaspoon allspice
¼	teaspoon ground cloves
½	teaspoon cinnamon
½	teaspoon ground ginger
1	tablespoon dark molasses
1	cup heavy cream
¼	cup rum (optional)

1. Whisk together the egg yolks and sugar in a large bowl until light yellow and creamy.

2. Add the milk and cinnamon stick to a large saucepan over medium heat and bring it to a simmer. Stir in the vanilla, salt, spices, and molasses until combined and warmed.

3. Slowly and carefully pour the hot mixture into the egg mixture a bit at a time, whisking briskly as you go.

4. Pour the combined mixture into the saucepan and cook over medium heat, stirring constantly, until the eggnog is thick and fluffy, about 5 minutes. (Don't let the liquid boil.)

5. Stir in the heavy cream and refrigerate the mixture for 4 hours or overnight. Stir in the rum before serving.

HOT APPLE CIDER FOR HIRE

Serves 6

*Enjoy while watching **Christmas Made to Order***

2018 – Starring Alexa PenaVega as Gretchen and Jonathan Bennett as Steven

What do you do when your sister asks you to host Christmas and you're woefully unprepared? Hire a beautiful stranger to deck the halls, of course! Gretchen specializes in Christmas spirit, so you know that her hot apple cider will hit the spot. Keep your mind in the moment (and off of work) by making it a family affair.

18	medium Gala apples, washed and cored
	Juice of 1 lemon
3	strips of orange peel, 1 inch wide each
1	cinnamon stick
3	cloves
	Half of a vanilla bean, split lengthwise

1. Cut the apples into slices, then add them to a large pot with just enough water to cover them. Bring the water to a low boil and cook the apples for 20–25 minutes until soft.

2. Line a fine-mesh strainer with a coffee filter or cheesecloth and place it over a large bowl. A bit at a time, ladle the apples and water into the strainer and gently press the apples against it to push their juice through. Discard the apple remains or reserve them for making applesauce.

   Note: You could also juice the apples using an electric juicer according to its instructions.

3. In a 4-quart saucepan, combine the juice with the remaining ingredients. Bring them to a boil over high heat, then reduce the heat to medium-low and let the mixture simmer for 30 minutes.

4. Pour the mulled cider through your fine-mesh strainer into a heat-safe serving bowl or pitcher and enjoy while hot.

A VERY MERRY CHEX MIX-UP

Serves 24

*Enjoy while watching **A Very Merry Mix-Up***

2013 – Starring Alicia Witt as Alice Chapman and Mark Wiebe as Matt Mitchum

This festive party mix is exactly the kind of indulgent snack that Christmas-lover Alice Chapman would make after finding her fiancé's healthy cereal in the cupboard. Luckily for her, a Christmas mix-up lands her with a family who can appreciate the sweeter things in life. Grab a bowl of this delicious mix and leave the tofu and green juice for someone else!

6	cups Rice Chex or Corn Chex cereal
2	cups mini marshmallows
1	cup mini pretzel twists
15	ounces vanilla candy coating
3	tablespoons red and green sprinkles
¼	cup powdered sugar
1	cup red and green candy-coated chocolates

1. In a large bowl, combine the cereal, marshmallows, and pretzels.

2. Break up the vanilla candy coating and add it to a medium-size microwavable bowl. Microwave on high for 60 seconds, then stir until smooth. (Microwave for an additional 30 seconds if necessary.)

3. Pour the candy coating over the cereal mixture and stir to coat.

4. Line a large rimmed cookie sheet with waxed paper. Spread the mixture evenly across the sheet, dust it with sprinkles, and let it cool completely (about 15 minutes).

5. Using your hands, break the mixture into bite-size pieces.

6. Add the pieces, powdered sugar, and candy-coated chocolates to a large resealable plastic food-storage bag, seal the bag, and shake to coat.

7. Serve in a large bowl, discarding any extra powdered sugar.

EDIBLE EGGNOG POPCORN ORNAMENTS

Serves 6

*Enjoy while watching **Coming Home for Christmas***

2017 – Starring Danica McKellar as Lizzie Richfield and Neal Bledsoe as Robert Marley

While decking the halls at the Ashford Estate, Lizzie shows the Marleys that some of the best Christmas decorations are homemade—and edible. She chooses plain popcorn chains to get the kids involved in the process, but these eggnog popcorn ornaments are on another level. They're as fitting for the Christmas Eve gala as they are for movie night in.

Nonstick cooking spray

1 cup granulated sugar

⅓ cup light corn syrup

⅓ cup cold water

1 teaspoon distilled white vinegar

¾ teaspoon fine salt

4 tablespoons unsalted butter, cut into small pieces

¾ teaspoon ground nutmeg

¾ teaspoon pure vanilla extract

9 cups plain popped popcorn

½ cup toasted pecans, coarsely chopped

1. Prepare a large, heat-safe bowl by greasing it with cooking spray. In a medium saucepan over high heat, combine the sugar, corn syrup, water, vinegar, and salt. Continue stirring until the sugar dissolves, about 2 minutes.

2. Bring the mixture to a boil and continue cooking until a candy thermometer reads 260°F, about 5–7 minutes. Remove the saucepan from the heat and stir in the butter, nutmeg, and vanilla until the butter is melted and the mixture is smooth.

3. In your prepared bowl, use a spatula to combine the popcorn, pecans, and hot mixture, stirring continuously until the popcorn is thoroughly coated and cool enough to handle.

4. Using greased hands, press the warm mixture into tight, 3-inch balls. Let the popcorn balls cool completely on wax paper, about 15–20 minutes.

HOLLY'S CHOCOLATE ENERGY CLUSTERS

Yield: 30 clusters

Enjoy while watching *Miss Christmas*

2017 – Starring Brooke D'Orsay as Holly Khun and Marc Blucas as Sam McNary

If you're like Holly Khun, Christmas is a marathon, not a sprint. Keep your energy up and your sweet tooth trained with these protein-packed chocolate bites. The best part is, these basically make themselves in your slow cooker so you can focus on finding the perfect Christmas tree.

1   (16-ounce) jar dry-roasted peanuts

1   (9.75-ounce) can salted whole cashews

2   cups pecan pieces

18 (2-ounce) chocolate bark coating squares, cut in half

1   (12-ounce) package semisweet chocolate morsels

4   (1-ounce) bittersweet chocolate baking squares, broken into pieces

1   tablespoon shortening

1   teaspoon pure vanilla extract

Red and green sprinkles (optional)

1. Combine the first 7 ingredients in a 5-quart slow cooker. Cover and cook on low for 2 hours or until the chocolate has melted.

2. Add the vanilla to the melted mixture and stir well to combine.

3. Drop the nut-filled chocolate by heaping teaspoonfuls onto wax paper. Top each with a dusting of your favorite holiday sprinkles.

4. Let the clusters stand until they are firm, about 2 hours. Eat them all immediately to cope with the stress, or store them in an airtight container.

NUTCRACKER'S DELIGHT (CANDIED WALNUTS)

Serves 4

Enjoy while watching *Christmas on Honeysuckle Lane*

2018 – Starring Alicia Witt as Emma Reynolds and Colin Ferguson as Morgan Shelby

Only a cozy Christmas movie can turn matching nutcrackers into a sign that two people are made for each other. When stubborn city girl Emma Reynolds went nutty for eccentric antique dealer Morgan Shelby, we all looked at those strange Christmas knick-knacks a little differently. But you're welcome to skip the antique nutcracker and use already halved walnuts for this recipe.

1	cup walnut halves/pieces
¼	cup granulated sugar
1	tablespoon unsalted butter

1. Add all of the ingredients to a nonstick skillet and cook over medium heat, stirring constantly, until the sugar has melted and the nuts are fully coated, about 5 minutes.

2. Transfer the nuts onto parchment paper and immediately separate them, moving quickly to avoid them setting in clusters. Allow the coating to set, about 5–7 minutes, before transferring the nuts to a serving bowl.

"Find the jolly."

—Tom White, *Finding Santa*

OLD-FASHIONED ROASTED CHESTNUTS

Serves 10

Enjoy while watching A Majestic Christmas

2018 – Starring Jerrika Hinton as Nell and Christian Vincent as Connor

The flavor of roasted chestnuts, especially when enjoyed with a special someone, is enough to make anyone a believer in Christmas traditions. Briar Falls native Nell uses that to her advantage while trying to show profit-centered Connor just how much Christmas magic is really worth. In the end, she proves to him that being a little old-fashioned can be a good thing.

16   ounces fresh chestnuts

Water, to boil

1. Using a serrated knife and holding the chestnuts down firmly, cut across the long side of each chestnut to make a slit in the shell.

2. Preheat the oven to 425°F. Add the chestnuts to a large pot of cold water and bring the water to a boil. Then use a slotted spoon to move the chestnuts to a rimmed baking sheet, placing them cut-side up in a single layer.

3. Roast the chestnuts in the oven for 15–20 minutes. Move them to a wire rack to cool for 10–15 minutes, and serve them slightly warm. Remove the shells just before eating the chestnuts to conserve their warmth.

CHRISTMASSY CANDY APPLES

Serves 4

Enjoy while watching *Christmas Under Wraps*

2014 – Starring Candace Cameron Bure as Dr. Lauren Brunell and David O'Donnell as Andy Holliday

An apple a day keeps the doctor away—especially when she's too busy to make it to the town's Christmas festival. If you're too busy too, you can bring the festivities home with these holiday-style candy apples. Dr. Brunell would be thrilled that at least half of your holiday treat is nutritious.

4	lollipop sticks
4	large apples, washed and thoroughly dried
	Nonstick cooking spray
1¼	cups granulated sugar
¼	cup corn syrup
¼	cup water
½	teaspoon red food coloring
1	cup white chocolate chips or melting wafers
	Crushed candy canes, for decoration

1. Line a baking sheet with parchment paper.

2. Insert a lollipop stick one-third of the way into each apple.

3. In a small saucepan, combine the sugar, corn syrup, and water, and bring the mixture to a boil. Reduce the heat to medium and stir in the food coloring.

4. Continue cooking, swirling the pan (don't stir the mixture), until a candy thermometer reads 290°F, about 10 minutes.

5. Remove the mixture from the heat. Immediately dip each apple into the candy to coat it, twirling off the excess before moving the apples to the baking sheet. Allow the candy to cool and set completely.

6. Add the white chocolate to a double boiler and melt it over low heat, stirring occasionally.

7. Dip the set apples into the chocolate to coat the bottom third of each, twirling off the excess. Immediately sprinkle the white chocolate with crushed candy canes. Allow the apples to set before eating them.

KATE'S BAKED CINNAMON SUGAR DOUGHNUTS

— Serves 6 —

*Enjoy while watching **Switched for Christmas***

2017 – Starring Candace Cameron Bure as Kate Lockhart and Chris Dixon, Eion Bailey as Tom Kinder, and Mark Deklin as Greg Turner

No Christmas festival would be complete without a handful of unhealthy treats, but kale-enthusiast Kate Lockhart may have needed convincing from her sister, Chris, when she took over planning Littleton's Winter Wonderland. These sweet doughnuts—which are baked, not fried—are the perfect compromise. Pair them with hot chocolate and a handsome companion.

Nonstick cooking spray
¾ cup flour
2 tablespoons cornstarch
⅓ cup sugar
1 teaspoon baking powder
½ teaspoon salt
½ teaspoon cinnamon
¼ teaspoon nutmeg
⅓ cup buttermilk
1 egg
1 tablespoon unsalted butter, melted
1 teaspoon vanilla

Topping

3 tablespoons unsalted butter, melted
1 teaspoon cinnamon
½ cup sugar

1. Lightly spray a six-doughnut pan with cooking spray.

2. In two separate bowls, whisk together the dry ingredients and whisk together the wet ingredients. Pour the wet mixture into the dry mixture and stir until just combined.

3. Spoon the batter into the doughnut pan, filling each well about two-thirds of the way up.

4. Bake at 375°F for 11–12 minutes. Move the doughnuts to a cooling rack.

5. Prepare the topping ingredients: have your melted butter ready and combine the cinnamon and sugar in a small bowl.

6. While they are still warm, brush each doughnut with melted butter, then dip it in the cinnamon sugar mixture until it's well coated. Serve immediately or store them in an airtight container for a few days.

KARLA'S POTATO AND SAUSAGE SOUP

Serves 6

Enjoy while watching *Let It Snow*

2013 – Starring Candace Cameron Bure as Stephanie Beck and Jesse Hutch
as Brady Lewis, plus Gabrielle Rose as Karla Lewis

Former Grinch Stephanie Beck would agree that one of the best things about Snow Valley Lodge is the food! Karla whips up all sorts of scrumptious creations, but this Swiss-inspired soup might be the coziest of all. Combine a piping-hot bowl with a blanket, a fireplace, and good friends for its full effect.

3	tablespoons unsalted butter
1	cup chopped onion
½	cup chopped celery
12–16	ounces smoked sausage, diced
¼	cup all-purpose flour
½	cup chopped green onion
1	tablespoon chopped fresh parsley or 1 teaspoon dried parsley flakes
1	teaspoon dried leaf basil
1	teaspoon kosher salt, or to taste
¼	teaspoon freshly ground black pepper
3	cups chicken broth
2	pounds baking potatoes, peeled and diced
1½	cups heavy cream

1. Melt the butter in a large, high-sided skillet or Dutch oven over medium-low heat. Add the onion, celery, and sausage and sauté until the sausage is lightly browned.

2. Add the flour to the sausage mixture and stir until well combined and smooth. Stir in the green onion, parsley, basil, salt, and pepper and cook while stirring for about 1 minute.

3. Stir in the chicken broth and diced potatoes, cover, and let the soup simmer for 25 minutes or until the potatoes are tender.

4. Stir in the heavy cream and continue cooking until the soup is heated through. Serve immediately.

NOT-FROM-THE-FOOD-COURT WONTON SOUP

Serves 4

Enjoy while watching *The Mistletoe Promise*

2016 – Starring Jaime King as Elise Donner and Luke Macfarlane as Nick Derr

Sometimes, the best holiday traditions are the ones you make yourself. Elise and Nick may start out as strangers, but a friendship forged in the food court over wonton soup changes everything. Now, no Christmas they share will be complete without that dumpling-filled dish.

Wontons

2/3	pound ground pork
2	teaspoons soy sauce
2	teaspoons thinly sliced chives
1	teaspoon rice wine vinegar
1	teaspoon cornstarch
1	teaspoon grated ginger
1	garlic clove
1/2	teaspoon crushed red pepper flakes
1/2	teaspoon sesame oil
1	package square wonton wrappers
1/4	cup water

Soup

4	cups chicken broth
1	(2-inch) piece ginger, peeled
2	teaspoons soy sauce
2	garlic cloves, smashed
1/4	teaspoon sesame oil
2	tablespoons sliced green onions, for garnish

For the wontons:

1. In a large bowl, mix together all of the wonton ingredients (except, of course, the wrappers and water) until well combined.

2. Lay out the wonton wrappers on a flat surface. Dip your finger into the water and wet the edges of one wonton wrapper.

3. Place a ½ tablespoon of your pork wonton filling in the center of the wrapper.

4. Fold the wrapper in half to create a triangle, and run your finger over the edges to seal them.

5. Fold the two sides of the triangle in toward the center of the wonton and press to seal them there.

6. Repeat steps 2–5 with the remaining wonton wrappers until you finish the pork filling.

For the soup:

1. Add all of the soup ingredients to a large pot over high heat and bring them to a boil.

2. Reduce the heat to low and let the soup simmer for 10 minutes.

3. Remove the garlic and ginger, then bring the soup back up to a boil.

4. Gently add the wontons to the soup and let them cook in the soup for 10 minutes. Serve the soup hot and garnished with green onions.

MULLIGAN STEW

Serves 8–10

Enjoy while watching *Crown for Christmas*

2015 – Starring Danica McKellar as Allie Evans and Rupert Penry-Jones as King Maximillian

Allie Evans has perfected the art of stretching a dollar into something hearty and delicious for her siblings (and the occasional royal butler) to enjoy. Her Mulligan Stew uses "everything in the kitchen, plus peas." The flavors of this inexpensive dish simmer together until each savory spoonful tastes like something from the Winshire palace kitchen.

¼	cup all-purpose flour
1	teaspoon freshly ground black pepper
1	pound beef stew meat, cut into 1-inch cubes
1	tablespoon olive or vegetable oil
2	(10½-ounce) cans beef broth
1	cup water
2	bay leaves
½	teaspoon garlic salt
½	teaspoon dried oregano
½	teaspoon dried basil

½	teaspoon dill weed
3	medium carrots, cut into 1-inch slices
2	medium potatoes, peeled and cubed
2	celery ribs, cut into 1-inch slices
1	medium onion, cut into eight wedges
1	cup each frozen corn, green beans, lima beans, and peas
1	tablespoon cornstarch
2	tablespoons cold water
1	tablespoon minced fresh parsley

1. Combine the flour and pepper in a large bowl or 1-gallon food-safe bag and toss the beef cubes in the mixture to coat them.

2. Heat the oil in a large pot over medium heat, then add the beef and sauté until lightly browned. Stir in the broth, water, bay leaves, and spices. Bring the mixture to a boil, then cover it, reduce the heat to low, and allow it to simmer until the meat is tender, about 2 hours.

3. Stir in the carrots, potatoes, celery, and onion, then replace the cover and simmer for 40 minutes. Then stir in the frozen vegetables, cover, and simmer until the vegetables are tender, about 15 minutes.

4. In a small bowl, combine the cornstarch and cold water until smooth. Stir this thickening mixture into the stew, then bring everything to a boil and continue to stir for 2 more minutes. Remove the bay leaves, stir in the parsley, and serve hot.

ZOE'S SNOWED-IN GRILLED CHEESE CASSEROLE

Serves 6

Enjoy while watching *Christmas in Evergreen*

2017 – Starring Ashley Williams as Allie Shaw and Teddy Sears as Ryan Bellamy, plus Jaeda Lily Miller as Zoe

When a whiteout grounds your flight, take a page out of Zoe's book and snuggle in with some cheesy comfort food. If they served this family-friendly casserole at the Kris Kringle diner, your little ones would be wishing for another helping!

3	ounces reduced-fat cream cheese
1½	teaspoons dried basil, divided
12	slices Italian bread (½-inch thick)
6	slices part-skim mozzarella cheese
6	tablespoons unsalted butter, softened
½	cup tomato paste
1	garlic clove, minced
¼	teaspoon kosher salt
¼	teaspoon freshly ground black pepper
1¾	cups 2% milk
2	large eggs
1	cup shredded Italian cheese blend or part-skim mozzarella cheese

1. Preheat the oven to 350°F. In a small bowl, combine the cream cheese and 1 teaspoon of the basil and spread the mixture onto 6 slices of the bread. Divide the mozzarella cheese evenly among the slices and top them each with the remaining bread slices. Butter the outsides of each sandwich before placing them in a 13 x 9-inch baking dish.

2. Add the tomato paste, garlic, salt, pepper, and remaining basil to a small saucepan and cook, while stirring, over medium heat for 1 minute. Slowly whisk in the milk, bring the mixture to a boil, then reduce the heat to low. Allow the mixture to simmer, stirring frequently, until it thickens, about 4–5 minutes. Remove the saucepan from the heat.

3. In a large bowl, whisk the eggs and then slowly add in the sauce mixture. Pour the sauce over the sandwiches in the baking dish. Top everything with an even sprinkling of shredded cheese and bake, uncovered, for 25–30 minutes or until it's golden brown with melted cheese. Let the casserole stand for 10 minutes before serving.

ROYAL CHRISTMAS TEA SANDWICHES

Yield: 12 sandwiches

Enjoy while watching A Princess for Christmas

2011 – Starring Katie McGrath as Jules Daly and Sam Heughan as Prince Ashton of Castlebury

We can't all be whisked off to castles near Leichtenstein to live like a royal for Christmas, but we can certainly up our snack game. This recipe turns Jules' "yummy" cucumber-and-watercress tea sandwiches into something that even Milo and Maddie would enjoy. If you need to save time, using canned or shredded rotisserie chicken works just as well as roasting one yourself.

3	boneless, skinless chicken breasts
3	tablespoons olive oil
	Kosher salt and freshly ground black pepper, to taste
¼	teaspoon dried thyme
2	ounces fresh cranberries, finely chopped
1	tablespoon mayonnaise
2	teaspoons Dijon mustard
1	pinch kosher salt
6	large slices white bread
1	bunch watercress
1	tablespoon unsalted butter

1. Preheat the oven to 350°F. Thoroughly rub the chicken breasts with olive oil, salt, pepper, and thyme, place them on a baking sheet, and bake for 25–30 minutes until a meat thermometer reads 165°F. Allow the chicken to cool before using two forks to shred it.

2. In a large bowl, mix together the shredded chicken, cranberries, mayonnaise, mustard, and salt.

3. Divide the mixture evenly among three slices of bread. Cover each with watercress.

4. Spread a thin layer of butter on one side of each of the remaining slices of bread and place them buttered-side down to create 3 sandwiches.

5. Cut off the crusts and slice each sandwich into 4 rectangular tea sandwiches before serving.

EMILY'S PHILLY-STYLE HOAGIE

──── Serves 4 ────

Enjoy while watching A Royal Christmas

2014 – Starring Lacey Chabert as Emily Taylor and Stephen Hagan as Prince Leopold

The only thing more iconic to Philadelphia than the cheesesteak is the Italian hoagie. So that's just what Emily Taylor makes when she decides to bring a little bit of Philly to a stuffy Cordinian ball. Whether or not to add pickles is a hot topic, but Emily thinks you can never have too many. Of course, she would tell you to be true to yourself!

2	(12-inch) Italian-style rolls
¼	pound thinly sliced boiled ham
¼	pound thinly sliced capicola
¼	pound thinly sliced provolone cheese
¼	pound thinly sliced Genoa salami
2	cups shredded iceberg lettuce
1	large tomato, thinly sliced
1	medium white onion, thinly sliced
	Hot and/or sweet peppers (optional)
2	tablespoons olive oil, divided
4	teaspoons red wine vinegar, divided
	Kosher salt and freshly ground black pepper, to taste
	Italian oregano, to taste

1. If the rolls are not pre-sliced, slice them lengthwise to the outer crust, leaving a hinge to create a cradle for the sandwich ingredients.

2. With the rolls lying open (cut-side up) on a counter or prep board, layer both with 4 slices each of the meats and cheese.

3. Top each open sandwich with a helping of lettuce, tomatoes, onions, and peppers (optional); half of the oil and vinegar; and salt, pepper, and oregano to taste.

4. Close the rolls, slice the sandwiches in half, and serve.

CHRISTMAS UNDER TURKEY WRAPS

Serves 2

Enjoy while watching *Christmas Under Wraps*

2014 – Starring Candace Cameron Bure as Dr. Lauren Brunell and David O'Donnell as Andy Holliday

Dr. Brunell would certainly approve of this healthy use of Christmas leftovers. And even she might have time to whip up one of these easy wraps between patients. Now, if she could just get Frank to try one. (Maybe if she promises him a cookie for dessert?)

2	(10-inch) tortillas or wraps
2	tablespoons sour cream
2	tablespoons grated Cheddar cheese
4	large lettuce leaves
½	medium butternut squash, cooked and diced
1	cup cooked and diced turkey
2	tablespoons cranberry sauce

1. Lightly toast the tortillas in a large frying pan over medium heat, about 1 minute on each side.

2. Spread half of the sour cream over each tortilla, leaving room at the edges to roll them up without cream spilling out. Divide the remaining ingredients evenly between the two tortillas.

3. Fold in the ends of each tortilla and roll them up tightly, tucking the ingredients in as you go. Cut the wraps in half and serve.

KRINGLE KITCHEN'S ROAST BEEF SPECIAL

Serves 8–10

Enjoy while watching *Christmas in Evergreen: Letters to Santa*

2018 – Starring Jill Wagner as Lisa and Mark Deklin as Kevin, plus Barbara Niven as Carol

Kringle Kitchen owner Carol might spend as much time fixing up people as she does fixing food. Luckily, she's great at both! The diner's oversized roast beef sandwiches are a hearty way to welcome friends and family into town for the holidays before the festivities (and intrigue) begin.

¼ cup extra-virgin olive oil

3 cloves garlic, minced

1 tablespoon chopped fresh rosemary

1 tablespoon chopped fresh thyme leaves

2 teaspoons kosher salt

1 teaspoon freshly ground black pepper

1 (4-pound) round roast

8–10 ciabatta rolls

Favorite toppings (lettuce, tomatoes, mustard, cheese, etc.)

1. Preheat the oven to 450°F. Combine the oil, garlic, rosemary, thyme, salt, and pepper in a small bowl. Rub the mixture all over the roast.

2. Place the beef in a roasting pan with a rack, and let it cook for 15 minutes. Reduce the heat to 325°F and continue roasting it for 1¾–2 hours until cooked to desired doneness.

3. Remove the roast from the oven and let it rest for 15–30 minutes before carving it and building your sandwiches.

CHAPTER 2:
CHRISTMAS GATHERINGS

—◦●◦—

HEALTHY HOLIDAY CRESCENT WREATH

Serves 16

*Enjoy while watching **Christmas in Love***

2018 – Starring Brooke D'Orsay as Ellie Hartman and Daniel Lissing as Nick Carlingson

This is exactly the sort of appetizer that creative entrepreneur-at-heart Ellie Hartman would bring to a holiday party. Her love of Christmas wreaths knows no bounds and would easily spill into the kitchen. Thankfully, this recipe features festive veggies to balance out all of those Carlingson Kringles.

2	(8-ounce) packages crescent rolls
½	cup packaged chive-and-onion cream cheese spread
2	cups finely chopped broccoli florets
6	slices bacon, cooked and crumbled
⅓	cup diced red bell pepper
1	large egg, beaten
1	teaspoon sesame seeds
	Fresh rosemary, for serving

"Christmas is beautiful, isn't it? Getting to be with the people that you care about, and sharing the traditions with the children."

—Maggie, *A Christmas to Remember*

1. Preheat the oven to 375°F. Unroll both packages of crescent rolls and separate the perforated triangles of dough. On an ungreased baking sheet, arrange the triangles in a sunburst with a 4-inch open circle in the center.

   Note: The triangle bases should overlap to create the outer edge of the circle while the points create the rays. The points may end up outside of the baking sheet.

2. Spread the cream cheese evenly over the widest part of the crescents to create a ring, leaving an inch between them and the circle's edge. Combine the broccoli, bacon, and bell pepper in a small bowl, then spread the mixture over the cream cheese.

3. Bring the points of the crescents over the filling, toward the open circle, and tuck them under the bases to secure the filling, which should still be visible.

4. Brush the dough with the beaten egg, then sprinkle it with sesame seeds.

5. Bake the ring for 20–25 minutes, or until golden brown and thoroughly baked. Allow it to cool slightly before slicing and serving, garnished with fresh rosemary.

BETTER-THAN-A-DIAMOND CRESCENT RING

Serves 16

Enjoy while watching *A Christmas Detour*

2015 – Starring Candace Cameron Bure as Paige Summerlind and Paul Greene as Dylan Smith

In one whirlwind weekend, Paige discovers that there's no recipe for finding a lasting relationship. Luckily, matchmaking in the kitchen is a lot easier. Cranberries and goat cheese are a perfect pair nestled inside buttery crescent rolls, creating a ring worthy of any vision board.

2	cups fresh cranberries
1	cup water
2	(8-count) packages crescent rolls
4	ounces crumbled goat cheese
½	cup honey
1	large egg, beaten
¼	cup almond slices
⅛	teaspoon cinnamon

1. Preheat the oven to 375°F. Add the cranberries and water to a small pot and cook over medium heat until the cranberry skins open, about 10 minutes. Remove the pot, drain the water, and set the cranberries aside.

2. Unroll both packages of crescent rolls and separate the perforated triangles of dough. On an ungreased baking sheet, arrange the triangles in a sunburst with a 4-inch open circle in the center.

   Note: The triangle bases should overlap to create the outer edge of the circle while the points create the rays. The points may end up outside of the baking sheet.

"Christmas is what you bake it."

— Betty, *Christmas Cookies*

3. Spread the softened cranberries evenly over the widest part of the crescents to create a ring, leaving an inch between them and the circle's edge. Sprinkle the goat cheese over the cranberries and drizzle the honey over the goat cheese.

4. Bring the points of the crescents over the filling, toward the open circle, and tuck them under the bases to secure the filling.

5. Brush the dough with the beaten egg, then sprinkle it with the almond slices and cinnamon.

6. Bake the ring for 20–25 minutes, or until golden brown and thoroughly baked. Allow it to cool slightly before serving.

SMASHED RED POTATOES

Serves 4

*Enjoy while watching **A Christmas to Remember***

2016 – Starring Mira Sorvino as Jennifer Wade (a.k.a. Maggie) and Cameron Mathison as Dr. John Blake

Sometimes you just smash into good things. Smash your car into a snowbank, fall in love with a handsome veterinarian. Smash some red potatoes, create a delicious and filling side dish or appetizer. The great thing about this recipe is that there are no measurements—just coat your potatoes in olive oil, herbs, and spices (and maybe a little parmesan cheese), and bake!

12 small red potatoes

Kosher salt

Olive oil, to coat

Dried basil, to taste

Dried thyme, to taste

Dried rosemary, to taste

Kosher salt and freshly ground black pepper, to taste

1. Bring a large pot of salted water to a boil. Add the potatoes and boil them for 15 minutes, or until they are fork-tender. Pour off the water and set the potatoes aside.

2. Preheat the oven to 450°F. Grease a baking sheet with olive oil and spread your potatoes evenly over it. Using a potato masher or fork, press down in the center of each potato to smash it.

3. Drizzle more olive oil over the potatoes, sprinkle them with the herbs and spices, and then use your hands to rub the herbs and spices all over the potatoes. Bake for 20 minutes or until the potatoes have browned.

DUCHESS OF WARREN POTATOES

Serves 6

Enjoy while watching A Royal Christmas

2014 – Starring Lacey Chabert as Emily Taylor and Stephen Hagan as Prince Leopold,
plus Katherine Flynn as Natasha

These creamy potatoes are an elegant spin on everyone's favorite appetizer: the potato. And with far less salt than Duchess Natasha, herself, you're bound to like these better than you like her.

---

2   pounds russet potatoes, peeled and quartered

3   large egg yolks

3   tablespoons fat-free milk

2   tablespoons butter

1   teaspoon kosher salt

¼   teaspoon freshly ground black pepper

⅛   teaspoon ground nutmeg

1   large egg, lightly beaten

1. In a large saucepan, cover the potatoes with water and bring it to a boil. Then reduce the heat, cover the pot, and let the potatoes simmer until tender, about 15–20 minutes.

2. Drain the potatoes and return them to the stove. Stir them over low heat until the steam evaporates, then remove the pan from the heat.

3. Preheat the oven to 400°F and line a baking sheet with parchment paper. Use a potato ricer or strainer to rice the potatoes into a large bowl. Stir in the egg yolks, milk, butter, salt, pepper, and nutmeg until well combined and creamy.

4. Add the potatoes to a pastry bag with a star tip, and pipe them into six mounds on your baking sheet. Brush each with beaten egg, then put them in the oven and let them bake for 20–25 minutes or until golden brown.

HOLIDAY-STYLE MEATBALLS

Serves 16

Enjoy while watching Hitched for the Holidays

2012 – Starring Joey Lawrence as Rob and Emily Hampshire as Julie

It wouldn't be Christmas at the Merinos without meatballs. Get your ingredients from a Kosher deli and these turkey meatballs will be a hit at any Hanukkah gathering. Just ask Rob and Julie—mixing holiday traditions is never easy. But done well, it can be delicious!

1   pound ground turkey

2   tablespoons finely diced dried cranberries

½   cup bread crumbs

1   tablespoon finely diced fresh sage

1   tablespoon finely diced fresh parsley

1   medium spring onion, finely diced

1   large egg, beaten

1   clove of garlic, minced

1   tablespoon olive oil, plus extra for cooking

1   teaspoon kosher salt

¼   teaspoon freshly ground black pepper

¼   teaspoon nutmeg

       Zest of ½ a small clementine or orange

       Olive oil

       Cranberry sauce (optional)

1. Add all of the ingredients to a large bowl and use your hands or a spatula to mix until just combined. (The less you work the mixture, the lighter your meatballs.) Roll the mixture into 16 evenly sized meatballs.

2. Grease a baking sheet with a little bit of olive oil and spread the meatballs evenly over it. Bake at 390°F for 15–20 minutes, turning the meatballs at the halfway point, until cooked through and golden brown. Serve them hot or cold with toothpicks and cranberry sauce for dipping.

BEN'S FAVORITE MUSHROOMS NEPTUNE

Yield: 45 mushrooms

Enjoy while watching *Family for Christmas*

2015 – Starring Lacey Chabert as Hannah Dunbar and Tyron Leitso as Ben Matthews

Impress your guests in any timeline with these delicious hors d'oeuvres! Ben's recipe for stuffed mushrooms may look complicated, but quick-thinking Hannah proves that even his kids can make it. (If you have little ones helping with the stuffing, don't worry about how the mushrooms look—they'll taste amazing.)

45	button mushrooms
1	tablespoon olive oil
1	pinch kosher salt
1	(8-ounce) package cream cheese, softened
2	tablespoons sour cream
2	teaspoons lemon juice
½	cup grated Swiss cheese
¼	cup grated Parmesan cheese
¾	teaspoon kosher salt
½	teaspoon freshly ground black pepper
½	cup finely chopped crabmeat
¼	cup cooked and finely chopped shrimp
3	green onions, minced

1. Wash the mushrooms and carefully remove the stems. Heat the olive oil in a large pan over medium-high heat. Add the mushroom caps, season them with salt, and sauté them for 2–3 minutes on each side until softened.

2. Preheat the oven to 400°F. In a large bowl, combine the rest of the ingredients.

3. Line a baking sheet with aluminum foil and sit a wire baking rack on top of it. Spread the mushroom caps evenly over the baking rack and fill each with the cream-cheese mixture.

4. Bake the mushrooms for 15 minutes, then broil them for 2–3 minutes until the tops have browned. Serve immediately.

LOBSTER MAC AND CHEESE

Serves 6–8

Enjoy while watching *A Dream of Christmas*

2016 – Starring Nikki Deloach as Penny and Andrew W. Walker as Stuart,
plus Lisa Durupt as Nicky and Paul Essiembre as Bryan

Like Nicky and Bryan, lobster and macaroni and cheese are "a match made in heaven…or Maine." This indulgent dish would surely please Penny's houseful of people. And considering Nicky's love of lobster, it's the least Penny could do for almost erasing her happily ever after.

	Kosher salt
1	tablespoon vegetable oil
1	pound cavatappi pasta or elbow macaroni
2	cups whole milk
2	cups heavy whipping cream
8	tablespoons unsalted butter, divided
½	cup all-purpose flour

4	cups shredded Gruyère cheese
2	cups shredded extra-sharp Cheddar
1	teaspoon kosher salt
½	teaspoon freshly ground black pepper
½	teaspoon nutmeg
1½	pounds cooked lobster meat
5	slices white bread, crumbed without crusts

"You're never too old to believe
in Christmas wishes."

–Kristin Parson, *A Christmas Melody*

1. Bring a large pot of water to a boil, then stir in the salt and oil. Add the pasta and cook it according to the directions on its package. Drain it well and set it aside.

2. Add the milk and heavy cream to a small saucepan, and heat it over low heat (don't let it boil). In a large pot over low heat, melt 6 tablespoons of the butter and stir in the flour. Cook and whisk the mixture for 2 minutes.

3. Continue whisking while you add the hot milk mixture. Let this cook until thickened and smooth, about 1–2 minutes. Remove the pot from the heat.

4. Preheat the oven to 375°F. Stir the cheese, 1 teaspoon of salt, pepper, and nutmeg into the large pot, followed by the cooked pasta and lobster, until everything is well combined.

5. Pour the lobster mac into a large casserole dish. In a small saucepan over low heat, combine the remaining butter and bread crumbs until the butter has melted and the mixture is crumbly. Sprinkle this evenly over the lobster mac.

6. Bake the lobster mac for 30–35 minutes, or until the sauce bubbles and the macaroni and bread crumbs have browned on top.

LEMONY SMOKED TROUT DIP

Serves 8

Enjoy while watching *Let It Snow*

2013 – Starring Candace Cameron Bure as Stephanie Beck and Jesse Hutch as Brady Lewis

Celebrating Christmas with the Feast of the Seven Fishes might feel more authentic when you live next to a frozen pond full of potential ingredients. But if you don't feel like ice-fishing for your own trout and smoking it (like a real Mainer), you can buy yours at the store. Serve this dip with crackers or toasted French bread for your starter.

12	ounces smoked trout, skin and bones removed
⅓	cup labneh (Lebanese strained yogurt) or Greek yogurt
¼	cup crème fraîche
1	tablespoon fresh lemon juice
3	tablespoons finely chopped fresh chives, plus more for serving
	Kosher salt and freshly ground black pepper, to taste
1	tablespoon olive oil
1	tablespoon finely chopped fresh dill, plus more for serving

1. In a medium bowl, use a fork to combine the trout, yogurt, crème fraîche, lemon juice, and chives until trout flakes into very small pieces. Season with salt and pepper.

2. Serve with a drizzle of olive oil and a sprinkling of chives and dill. Refrigerate for up to 2 days.

VERMONT MAPLE BACON DIP

Serves 16

Enjoy while watching *Last Vermont Christmas*

2018 – Starring Erin Cahill as Megan Marvin and Justin Bruening as Nash

Make the final Christmas in your childhood home hurt a bit less with this comfort-food dip, which features everything that's great about Vermont. It's so good you just might choose to stick around a little longer.

1 (8-ounce) package cream cheese, softened

½ cup mayonnaise

½ cup 2% milk

8 slices bacon, cooked and crumbled

1 package gravy mix

1½ cups shredded sharp Cheddar cheese, divided

Nonstick cooking spray

⅓ cup chopped red apple

2 tablespoons Vermont maple syrup, for serving

1. Preheat the oven to 350°F. In a large bowl, mix together the cream cheese, mayonnaise, milk, bacon, gravy, and 1 cup of the cheese until well combined.

2. Grease a 9-inch pie plate with cooking spray and pour your dip mixture into it, spreading it evenly. Top it with the remaining ½ cup of cheese and the apple.

3. Bake for 25 minutes or until the dip is heated through and the cheese has melted. Serve warm, topped with a drizzle of a maple syrup.

CRANBERRY BRIE BITES

Yield: 24 bites

Enjoy while watching *Merry Matrimony*

2015 – Starring Jessica Lowndes as Brie Traverston and Christopher Russell as Eddie Chapman

Busy art director Brie Traverston would delight in the beauty of these namesake hors d'oeuvres. But between angling for a partner and falling in love with her college sweetheart all over again, she doesn't have time to make puff pastry. Thankfully, packaged crescent rolls are just as delicious.

Nonstick cooking spray

Flour

1 (8-ounce) package crescent roll dough

1 (8-ounce) wheel Brie

½ cup whole-berry cranberry sauce

¼ cup chopped pecans

6 sprigs of rosemary, cut into 1-inch pieces

1. Preheat the oven to 375°F and grease 2 mini muffin pans with cooking spray. On a lightly floured surface, roll out the crescent dough and pinch together seams.

2. Cut the dough into 24 squares and place one square into each muffin cup.

3. Cut the Brie into small pieces (larger pieces will spill over when cooked) and place one inside each of the dough squares. Top each with a spoonful of cranberry sauce, some chopped pecans, and a small sprig of rosemary.

4. Bake the Brie bites until the pastry is golden, about 15 minutes. Serve hot.

A ROYAL CHEESE BALL

— Serves 6 —

Enjoy while watching *A Princess for Christmas*

2011 – Starring Katie McGrath as Jules Daly and Sam Heughan as Prince Ashton of Castlebury

"Unsuitable Americans" and royals alike can appreciate this bejeweled treat. Not only is it as beautiful to look at as a long-forgotten royal ball, it's also yummy enough for the whole family to enjoy. Maddie might even put down her potato chips for a taste!

2	tablespoons unsalted butter
10	fresh sage leaves
1	(8-ounce) package cream cheese, softened
4	ounces mascarpone cheese, softened
6	ounces freshly grated sharp white Cheddar cheese
½	cup slivered almonds, toasted
¼	teaspoon kosher salt
¼	teaspoon freshly ground black pepper
1	cup pomegranate seeds
	Crackers, for serving

1. Add the butter to a small skillet over medium heat and allow it to melt and begin to sizzle. Add in the sage leaves and cook for about 1 minute per side, until crisp. Move the leaves to a paper towel and set the remaining butter aside.

2. Use an electric mixer on low to combine the cheeses in a large bowl. Mix in the almonds, sage leaves, butter, salt, and pepper until well combined, about 1 minute, using a spatula to scrape the sides as necessary.

3. Mold the mixture into a large cheese ball, then roll it in plastic wrap and move it to the refrigerator to set for about 30 minutes.

4. Pat the seeds dry on a paper towel.

5. After 30 minutes, take the cheese ball out of the refrigerator and smooth it out if needed. Pour the seeds onto a dinner plate and roll the ball through them, using your hands to press the seeds in so that they stick and cover the surface of the ball completely. Serve immediately or refrigerate for up to 2 days.

EMMA'S SNOWMAN CHEESEBALL

Serves 6

Enjoy while watching *Christmas at Grand Valley*

2018 – Starring Danica McKellar as Kelly and Brennan Elliott as Leo plus Hattie Kragten as Emma

Kelly's approach to teaching the Christmas camp at the Grand Valley Lodge has a lot to do with building and painting snowmen. But kids need snacks to keep their creative juices flowing. What better than a snack that requires a bit of childlike wonder? There's even a zucchini-ribbon scarf just for Emma.

Day 1

2	(8-ounce) packages cream cheese, softened
4	ounces deli-style roast beef, chopped
½	cup finely chopped green onions
1	teaspoon prepared horseradish
½	teaspoon garlic powder
½	cup dried parsley flakes

Day 2

2	(4-ounce) cartons spreadable cream cheese
5	dried cranberries
1	baby carrot
2	pretzel sticks
4	round butter-flavored crackers
1	large round cracker
1	long zucchini ribbon (optional)
	More crackers, for serving

"Christmas is a time to come together.
It's about family, giving, and love."

—King Max, *Crown for Christmas*

1. Add the softened cream cheese to a large bowl, and use an electric mixer to beat it on medium speed until smooth. Stir in the roast beef, green onions, horseradish, and garlic powder until well combined.

2. Shape the cream-cheese mixture into two balls that will create the body of your snowman, setting aside 1 tablespoon of it and refrigerating it for the next day. Pour the parsley flakes onto a plate, and roll the cheeseballs in the flakes until well covered. Cover the balls with plastic wrap and move them to the refrigerator to set overnight.

3. When you're ready to serve, build your snowman on a serving plate. Unwrap the cheese balls and place them one on top of the other. Carefully spread the spreadable cream cheese over the whole snowman.

4. Use the cranberries to create two eyes and three buttons. Cut the baby carrot to create a nose, and insert a pretzel stick on each side for arms.

5. To create the snowman's hat, stack the 4 butter-flavored crackers on top of the larger round cracker, spreading a bit of the reserved cream-cheese mixture in between each. Use a little dab of the mixture to adhere the hat to the snowman's head.

6. Finish your snowman with a zucchini-ribbon scarf and serve him with plenty of crackers.

NOELLE'S COCKTAIL DOGS

Yield: 20 franks

Enjoy while watching *A Shoe Addict's Christmas*

2018 – Starring Candace Cameron Bure as Noelle Carpenter, Luke Macfarlane
as Jake Marsden, and Jean Smart as Charlie

Charlie might have put Noelle on the right path, but she also taught us that a little timeline jumping never hurt anybody. In Noelle's other life as the owner of a successful chain of hot dog carts, she certainly would have served guests some of her wares in this tasty sweet-and-sour sauce.

1   (1-pound) package cocktail franks

1   cup yellow mustard

3   cups grape jelly

1. Add all of the ingredients to a 6-quart slow cooker, adjusting the sour-to-sweet ratio by adding more or less mustard or jelly.

2. Cook the mixture on low for 3–4 hours, stirring occasionally. Serve warm.

   Note: You can serve the franks straight from the slow cooker to keep them warm.

MARIE'S CHRISTMAS TREE PIZZAS

Yield: 24 pizzas

Enjoy while watching *12 Gifts of Christmas*

2015 – Starring Katrina Law as Anna Parisi and Aaron O'Connell as Marc Rehnquist, plus Melanie Nelson as Marie

As a busy mom and maker of the best pizza in town, Marie knows how to play to her strengths. If her daughters' school asks her to prepare a holiday-themed snack, these little trees would be a no-brainer! Don't be afraid to get creative with the pizza toppings. Like her sister, Anna, Marie encourages people to think outside the box.

---

1   (12-ounce) frozen puff pastry sheet

1   large tree-shaped cookie cutter

4   tablespoons favorite pizza sauce

4½   ounces grated mozzarella cheese

3   pepperoni snack sticks, sliced into tiny pepperoni

1   medium green pepper, sliced into small strips

1. Thaw and unfold the puff pastry. Use your cookie cutter to cut out as many trees as you can from the dough and spread them evenly over a baking sheet (or two) lined with baking paper.

2. Preheat the oven to 400°F. Create your mini pizzas by topping each tree with pizza sauce, cheese, and a smattering of green peppers and pepperoni.

3. Bake the pizzas for 10 minutes or until the pastry is puffed and golden brown, and serve them immediately.

PUPPY CHOW (A.K.A. MUDDY BUDDIES)

Serves 15

Enjoy while watching ***Dashing through the Snow***

2015 – Starring Meghan Ory as Ashley Harrison and Andrew W. Walker as Dash Sutherland

You know what's better than meeting a kind and handsome stranger and adopting an adorable stray puppy all in the same day? Snacking on this ridiculously delicious chocolate-peanut-butter Chex mix while you wind your way over back roads to Seattle. Having this protein-rich snack in your stomach might even help with motion sickness. (Just don't let Little Blade have any—the chocolate in this "puppy chow" is bad for dogs.)

1	cup semisweet chocolate chips
1	cup creamy peanut butter
6–7	cups Rice Chex cereal
1–2	cups powdered sugar

"Every Christmas, I would go someplace new. But no matter where I went, there it was. That Christmas energy. There's no escaping it. Which is a good thing, because it makes the world a better place. Not so separate."

—Eddie Chapman, *Merry Matrimony*

1. Add the chocolate and peanut butter to a medium saucepan and let it melt over low heat, stirring occasionally.

2. In a large bowl, gently combine 3 cups of cereal with 1 cup of your melted chocolate peanut butter. Add 3 more cups of cereal to the bowl, followed by the rest of the chocolate peanut butter. Gently stir until the cereal is evenly coated.

   Note: If you have a lot of excess chocolate peanut butter, add more cereal to the mixture ¼ cup at a time until most of the excess has been used. You want some chocolatey clumps, so err on the side of less cereal.

3. Allow the mixture to come just to room temperature before adding 1 cup of powdered sugar and mixing until combined. Alternatively, you can add the cereal and sugar to a large food-safe bag and shake until combined. Add more powdered sugar to coat, if necessary.

4. Let the puppy chow cool for 15 minutes before serving it or packing it into an airtight container and storing it at room temperature.

SMALL WORLD STICKY BUNS

Serves 16

Enjoy while watching *Journey Back to Christmas*

2016 – Starring Candace Cameron Bure as Hanna and Oliver Hudson as Jake

While nurse Hanna learns what a small world it is and how much of an impact one person can have, she wouldn't mind a few of the comforts of home. Sticky buns are a warm and inviting breakfast treat that spans centuries, so they are perfect for an unexpected guest who drops in from the forties. This recipe keeps things simple, the way Hanna prefers, with prepackaged dough and an overnight rise.

1	cup unsalted butter, melted
¼	cup honey
1	cup light brown sugar, divided
1	cup chopped toasted pecans
½	cup raisins or other dried fruit (optional)
2	(1-pound) loaves frozen bread dough, defrosted
1	teaspoon ground cinnamon

1. Add the butter to a medium saucepan and let it melt over medium heat. Set aside ½ cup of the melted butter.

2. Stir the honey and ½ cup of the brown sugar into the saucepan, then bring the mixture to a boil. The sugar should dissolve.

3. Pour the mixture into a 9 x 13-inch baking dish. Evenly distribute the nuts and fruit over the mixture.

4. Roll one of the loaves of room-temperature dough onto a lightly floured surface to create a 12 x 8-inch rectangle. Brush the dough with ½ of the reserved butter, leaving 1 inch unbuttered at the long edge farthest from you.

5. In a small bowl, combine the brown sugar and cinnamon. Sprinkle half of the cinnamon sugar over the buttered dough.

6. Starting with the long edge closest to you, tightly roll the dough into a log, pinching the edges closed at the end. Slice the log evenly into 8 rolls.

7. Repeat steps 4–6 with the second loaf of dough. Place the cinnamon rolls cut-side up into the baking dish so that they sit in the sticky mixture. Cover the dish with plastic wrap and refrigerate it overnight to let the dough rise.

8. In the morning, let the dish sit on the countertop for 1½ hours to rise and come to room temperature. Preheat the oven to 350°F and bake for 30 minutes until the buns are golden brown.

9. Let the buns rest for 5 minutes before turning them out, upside down, onto a large platter. Scrape any remaining sticky mixture out of the dish and onto the buns. Serve immediately.

ISOBEL'S DANCING SUGARPLUMS

—— *Yield: 80 sugarplums* ——
Enjoy while watching **Christmas List**

2016 – Starring Alicia Witt as Isobel Gray and Gabriel Hogan as Jamie Houghton

If making traditional sugarplums isn't on your Christmas to-do list right next to singing carols and decorating a real tree, it should be. Filled with healthy fruit to balance out the sugar, these little treats are perfect for the little sugarplum fairies in your life.

6	ounces slivered almonds, toasted
4	ounces dried plums
4	ounces dried apricots
4	ounces dried figs
¼	cup powdered sugar
¼	teaspoon anise seeds, toasted
¼	teaspoon fennel seeds, toasted
¼	teaspoon caraway seeds, toasted
¼	teaspoon ground cardamom
1	pinch kosher salt
¼	cup honey
1	cup coarse sugar

1. Add the almonds, plums, apricots, and figs to a food processor and pulse until everything is well chopped but not combined.

2. In a medium bowl, combine the powdered sugar, anise, fennel, caraway, cardamom, and salt. Add the fruit mixture and the honey to the mixture, and use your hands to mix everything together.

3. Roll the mixture into roughly 80 ¼-ounce balls. Just before serving, roll each ball in coarse sugar.

   Note: Sugarplums get better as they dry out, so don't be afraid to let them sit out for up to a week. After that, store them in an airtight container for up to 1 month.

NO-NONSENSE BUTTERMILK PANCAKES

Serves 8

Enjoy while watching *A Royal Christmas*

2014 – Starring Lacey Chabert as Emily Taylor and Stephen Hagan as Prince Leopold

These fluffy pancakes are fit for a prince! Without all that fruit or chocolate nonsense, original homemade pancakes really shine. Serve them up with a side of bacon (if His Royal Highness hasn't eaten it all).

2	cups all-purpose flour
3	tablespoons sugar
2	teaspoons baking powder
½	teaspoon baking soda
½	teaspoon kosher salt
2¼	cups buttermilk
2	large eggs, lightly beaten at room temperature
1	teaspoon pure vanilla extract
4	tablespoons unsalted butter, melted and cooled
	Nonstick cooking spray

1. In a large bowl, whisk together all of the dry ingredients until well combined.

2. In another large bowl, whisk together the buttermilk, eggs, and vanilla. Slowly whisk in the melted butter until everything is well combined.

3. Stir the wet ingredients into the dry ingredients until just combined, being careful not to overmix. Preheat a large skillet over medium heat and spray it with cooking spray.

4. Once the skillet is hot, pour the batter in as many rounds as will fit, ½–⅔ cup at a time. Cook each until the edges begin to brown and the bubbles in the batter begin to burst. Carefully flip the pancakes and continue cooking until they are golden brown on both sides. Repeat this process with the remaining batter until you have a stack of warm, golden pancakes ready to serve.

FRANK'S CHRISTMAS PANCAKES

Serves 8

Enjoy while watching *Christmas at Grand Valley*

2018 – Starring Danica McKellar as Kelly and Brennan Elliott as Leo, plus Dan Lauria as Frank

The inspiration goes both ways in Grand Valley—Kelly fills Leo and his kids with Christmas spirit, and they, in turn, inspire Frank to add some holiday fun to his everyday menu. Christmas Pancakes, or "the Grand Valley Special," turn scrumptious strawberries into festive decorations. You can even eat them for dinner!

1	cup all-purpose flour
2	tablespoons brown sugar
2	teaspoons baking powder
1	teaspoon kosher salt
1	cup 2% milk
2	tablespoons vegetable oil
1	large egg
2	tablespoons pure vanilla extract
1	cup chopped fresh strawberries
	Nonstick cooking spray
	Sliced strawberries, for serving
	Whipped cream, for serving

1. Combine the flour, brown sugar, baking powder, and salt in a large bowl. Stir in the milk, oil, egg, and vanilla until well combined, then stir in the strawberries. (For light, fluffy pancakes, make sure not to overmix.)

2. Preheat a large skillet or griddle over medium heat and grease it with cooking spray. Pour the batter into as many pancakes as you can fit and flip them as they begin to bubble in the center. Continue cooking them until they are golden brown on both sides. Repeat the process with the remaining batter.

3. Add one or two pancakes to a plate and arrange sliced strawberries to create a Santa hat and whipped cream to create the hat's fur trim and Santa's beard. Serve with your favorite syrup.

HOLLY'S EGGNOG FRENCH TOAST

Serves 6

Enjoy while watching *Miss Christmas*

2017 – Starring Brooke D'Orsay as Holly Khun and Marc Blucas as Sam McNary

Surprise your loved ones with a fresh truce, a messy kitchen, and the smell of breakfast on the stove. A little eggnog and some help from family and new friends turn this simple breakfast into a dish worthy of Christmas morning.

Nonstick cooking spray

1½ cups nonalcoholic eggnog

5 large eggs

½ teaspoon ground nutmeg

½ teaspoon rum extract

12 slices Texas toast or French bread

Maple syrup, for serving

1. Heat a large skillet over medium heat, and spray it with cooking spray.

2. In a large mixing bowl, whisk together the eggnog, eggs, nutmeg, and rum extract.

3. Dip the bread, one slice at a time, into the eggnog mixture once on each side to coat. Gently shake off any excess before moving the bread to the skillet. (Only dip as many slices as can fit in the skillet at one time so as not to oversoak them.)

4. Cook each slice until the bottom of the bread is golden, then flip it and cook until the other side is golden. Serve warm with maple syrup.

KATE'S EASY BREAKFAST CASSEROLE

—— Serves 8 ——

*Enjoy while watching **Switched for Christmas***

2017 – Candace Cameron Bure as Kate Lockhart and Chris Dixon, Eion Bailey as Tom Kinder, and Mark Deklin as Greg Turner

While Chris knew how to put a big, hearty breakfast on the table for her ravenous teenage children, twin sister Kate might have been better off with this simple casserole. If, like Kate, you tend to test the smoke detectors when cooking bacon, try using the oven instead of the stove.

2	(9-ounce) packages breakfast sausage links
1	pound bacon
	Nonstick cooking spray
1	(32-ounce) package tater tots
12	large eggs
½	cup whole milk
¼	cup green onions thinly sliced
½	teaspoon kosher salt
¼	teaspoon freshly ground black pepper
1	cup shredded Monterey jack cheese, shredded
2	cups shredded Cheddar cheese, divided
	Sliced green onions, for garnish

"Never, ever postpone the chance
for joy if you get it."

—Emory Blake, *Christmas Getaway*

1. In a large skillet over medium heat, heat the sausages until cooked through and slightly browned. Move the cooked sausages to a paper towel–lined plate and drain the skillet. Slice the sausages into ½-inch pieces.

2. In the same skillet, cook the bacon until brown and crisp. Let the bacon cool and drain on a paper towel–lined plate before crumbling it and setting it aside.

3. Preheat the oven to 350°F and spray a 9 x 13-inch baking dish with cooking spray. Create a single layer of tater tots in the bottom of the dish.

4. In a large bowl, whisk together the eggs, milk, green onions, salt, and pepper. Stir in the cooked sausage and ½ of the crumbled bacon, followed by the Monterey jack cheese, and 1 cup of the Cheddar cheese.

5. Pour the egg mixture over the tater tots and bake for 40–45 minutes, until the egg has set. Sprinkle the remaining Cheddar cheese evenly over the casserole, and return it to the oven for an additional 5–7 minutes until it has melted.

6. Let the casserole stand for 10 minutes before slicing and serving it, topped with the remaining crumbled bacon and a few slices of green onion.

A TURKEY TO REMEMBER

Serves 10

Enjoy while watching *A Christmas to Remember*

2016 – Starring Mira Sorvino as Jennifer Wade (a.k.a. Maggie) and Cameron Mathison as Dr. John Blake

This recipe is Christmas-dinner perfection worthy of food-and-style guru Jennifer Wade! But don't have a meltdown if your turkey doesn't turn out flawless—it will still taste delicious. (Maybe carry the turkey in from the kitchen yourself. Just as a precaution.)

1	(15-pound) turkey, thawed if frozen
	Kosher salt and freshly ground black pepper, to taste
1	medium onion, peeled and quartered
1	medium lemon, quartered
	Several whole sprigs of herbs (sage, rosemary, and thyme)
10	tablespoons unsalted butter, softened
2	teaspoons minced garlic
2	tablespoons finely chopped fresh sage leaves
1	tablespoon finely chopped fresh rosemary
2	tablespoons finely chopped fresh thyme leaves
¼	cup finely chopped fresh parsley leaves
	Kosher salt and freshly ground black pepper, to taste
3	cups chicken or turkey broth

1. Let the turkey stand at room temperature for 30 minutes, then tuck the turkey wings under the body of the bird.

2. Preheat the oven to 450°F. Season the cavity of the bird with salt and pepper, then place the onion, lemon, and whole herbs inside. Use kitchen twine to tie the turkey legs together in front of the cavity.

3. In a food processor, blend together the butter, garlic, sage, rosemary, thyme, parsley, salt, and pepper until smooth. Rub the herb butter into the turkey, both under and over the skin.

4. Place the turkey in a roasting pan, put it in the oven, and let it roast for 45 minutes.

5. Warm the chicken broth in a medium saucepan over low heat. Reduce the oven temperature to 350°F and continue roasting for another 3 hours, basting the turkey with the warm broth every 30 minutes, until the internal temperature of the thickest part of the turkey thigh reaches 165°F.

   Note: If the turkey starts getting too dark, cover it with aluminum foil.

6. Let the turkey rest (loosely covered with foil) for 25 minutes before slicing and serving it.

AUNT JANE'S CRANBERRY ORANGE SCONES

Yield: 10 scones
Enjoy while watching *A Godwink Christmas*

2018 – Starring Kimberly Sustad as Paula Mayer, Paul Campbell as Gery Conover, and Kathie Lee Gifford as Aunt Jane

A cold New England Christmas calls for a cup of tea and some yummy baked goods, neither of which hurt to have around when you're trying to decide if you're engaged to the wrong guy. If he doesn't make you as happy as these sugar-glazed scones do, you might just have your answer.

Scones

1	cup dried cranberries
¼	cup orange juice
¼	cup half-and-half cream
1	large egg, room temperature
2	cups all-purpose flour
1	tablespoon grated orange zest
2	teaspoons baking powder
½	teaspoon kosher salt
¼	teaspoon baking soda
10	teaspoons granulated sugar, divided
⅓	cup cold unsalted butter
1	tablespoon whole milk

Glaze

½	cup powdered sugar
1	tablespoon orange juice

1. Combine the cranberries, orange juice, cream, and egg in a small bowl.

2. In a large bowl, stir together the flour, orange zest, baking powder, salt, baking soda, and 7 teaspoons of the sugar. Use a pastry blender or a fork to cut in the butter.

3. Preheat the oven to 400°F. Stir the cranberry mixture into the flour mixture until a soft dough forms. Gently knead the dough 6–8 times on a lightly floured surface, then pat it into an 8-inch circle. Cut the dough into 10 even wedges.

4. Place the wedges on a greased baking sheet. Brush them with milk and dust them with the remaining sugar. Bake the scones for 12–15 minutes until they are lightly browned, then move them to a wire rack.

5. Mix together the glaze ingredients and drizzle the glaze over the scones before serving them warm.

TURKEY POT PIE FROM LUKE'S TABLE

Serves 6

Enjoy while watching *Pride, Prejudice, and Mistletoe*

2018 – Starring Lacey Chabert as Darcy Fitzwilliam and Brendan Penny as Luke Bennett

Luke's need to be right may get annoying at times, but Darcy can't debate his culinary know-how. His catering menu of honey-roasted figs and pancetta-wrapped tenderloin sounds mouthwatering! Since we can't all be talented cooks-turned-caterers, this version of his Turkey Pot Pie takes a few shortcuts.

1	(14.1-ounce) package refrigerated pie crusts, softened
⅓	cup unsalted butter
⅓	cup chopped onion
⅓	cup all-purpose flour
½	teaspoon kosher salt
¼	teaspoon freshly ground black pepper
1	(14-ounce) can chicken broth
½	cup 2% milk
2½	cups cooked and shredded turkey
2	cups frozen mixed vegetables, thawed

1. Preheat the oven to 425°F and line a 9-inch glass pie plate with one of the pie crusts.

2. Melt the butter in a medium saucepan over medium heat. Add the onion and cook while stirring for 2 minutes until the onion is tender.

3. Stir in the flour, salt, and pepper until well combined, then slowly stir in the broth and milk. Continue cooking and stirring until the mixture thickens and bubbles.

4. Stir the turkey and mixed vegetables into the broth mixture, then remove the saucepan from the heat. Spoon the finished filling into the crust-lined pie plate. Top with the second crust and use your fingers or a fork to seal the edges. Cut several slits in the top crust to allow the steam to vent.

5. Bake your pot pie for 30–40 minutes until the crust is golden brown. If the edges of the pie begin to get too dark, cover them with strips of aluminum foil. Let the pie stand for 5 minutes before serving.

ENGAGEMENT CHICKEN

——— *Serves 2–4* ———

Enjoy while watching ***Engaging Father Christmas***

2017 – Starring Erin Krakow as Miranda Chester and Niall Matter as Ian McAndrick

This recipe has a reputation for leading to an engagement ring, but cozy Christmas movie heroines don't usually have a problem in that area. All Miranda had to do was fly cross-country to Vermont and check into the cozy Carlton Heath Inn to bewitch her future fiancé. (Come to think of it, roasting this chicken might be less work.)

———

1	(4-pound) whole chicken
½	cup fresh lemon juice
3	medium lemons, divided
1	tablespoon kosher salt
½	teaspoon freshly ground pepper
	Fresh herbs for garnish (rosemary, sage, thyme)

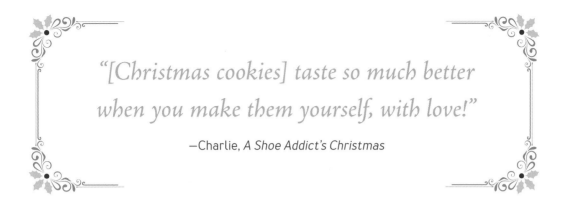

"[Christmas cookies] taste so much better when you make them yourself, with love!"

—Charlie, *A Shoe Addict's Christmas*

1. Place the oven rack in the upper third of the oven and preheat the oven to 400°F. Remove all contents from the cavity of the chicken and rinse the chicken—inside and out—with cold water. Let the chicken drain, cavity down, for 2 minutes.

2. Use paper towels to pat the chicken dry, then place it breast-side down in a medium roasting pan with a rack. Pour the lemon juice over and inside the chicken, then season it with salt and pepper inside and out.

3. Roll 2 of the lemons against your counter to loosen up the juices, then use a fork to pierce each three times to vent. Put them as deep inside the cavity as possible.

4. Lower the oven temperature to 350°F and roast the chicken, uncovered, for 15 minutes. Take the chicken out of the oven and, using tongs or utensils, turn it breast-side up. Insert an oven-safe meat thermometer into the thickest portion of the thigh (making sure not to hit bone) and return the chicken to the oven.

5. Roast the chicken for 1–1¼ hours, or until the thermometer reads 180°F and the juices run clear when you pierce the thigh. Let the chicken stand for 10 minutes before carving. Slice the remaining lemon. Pour the cooking juices over the sliced chicken and serve it garnished with the herbs and lemon slices.

ISADORA'S ORANGE DUCK

Serves 4–6

Enjoy while watching A Royal Christmas

2014 – Starring Lacey Chabert as Emily Taylor and Stephen Hagan as Prince Leopold,
plus Jane Seymour as Queen Isadora

While any of the elegant dishes on Queen Isadora's table would make a lovely Christmas dinner (minus, maybe, the jellied eels and haggis), Orange Duck may be the most scrumptious. If you're intimidated by the idea of roasting a duck, channel Emily's indomitable spirit and give it a try.

Duck

1	(6.2-ounce) package fast-cooking long grain and wild rice mix
1	(6-pound) domestic duck
¼	cup thawed orange juice concentrate
3	tablespoons honey
2	tablespoons unsalted butter, melted
2	tablespoons soy sauce

Orange Sauce

¼	cup thawed orange juice concentrate
1	cup water
1	tablespoon cornstarch
2	tablespoons cold water
⅛	teaspoon kosher salt

1. Prepare the rice according to the directions on the package and loosely stuff the duck with it. Use a fork to pierce the skin of the duck in several places. Skewer the neck opening and use kitchen twine to tie the legs together.

2. Preheat the oven to 350°F. In a small bowl, combine the orange juice concentrate, honey, butter, and soy sauce and set the mixture aside for basting.

3. Place the duck breast-side up in a roasting pan with a rack. Bake it, uncovered, for 1 hour, then baste it with the juice mixture. Continue baking it for another 1½–2 hours, basting occasionally, until a meat thermometer reads 180°F in the thigh of the duck and 165°F in the stuffing.

   Note: You can drain the fat from the pan as it accumulates. If the duck browns too much, you can cover it loosely with foil for the remaining cooking time.

4. Remove the duck from the oven, cover it loosely, and let it stand for 20 minutes before removing the stuffing to a serving dish and carving and serving topped with orange sauce. (Discard any remaining juice mixture.)

For the sauce:

1. Combine the orange juice concentrate and water in a small saucepan over medium heat and bring it to a boil.

2. In a small bowl, stir together the cornstarch and 2 tablespoons cold water until smooth. Add this to the saucepan and continue cooking and stirring for 2 minutes until the sauce thickens. Stir in the salt before serving.

CRANBERRY-STUFFED CROWN ROAST

—— *Serves 12* ——

Enjoy while watching *Crown for Christmas*

2015 – Starring Danica McKellar as Allie Evans and Rupert Penry-Jones as Prince Maximillian

Consummate cook Allie Evans would have no problem whipping up this elegant roast, which is fit for a king yet yummy enough to impress his picky little princess. Whether or not she makes it, we know that Allie is headed for a crown of her own—all thanks to a chance meeting and a sewing kit.

1	teaspoon granulated sugar
½	teaspoon dried thyme
½	teaspoon freshly ground black pepper
1	(7-pound) pork crown roast with 12 ribs
¼	cup unsalted butter
¾	cup chopped celery
½	cup chopped onion
5	cups cubed day-old bread
1	cup chicken broth
⅔	cup cooked long grain rice
½	cup cooked wild rice
⅓	cup chopped fresh cranberries
¼	cup minced fresh parsley
2	tablespoons light brown sugar
1	tablespoon Worcestershire sauce
2	teaspoons poultry seasoning
½	teaspoon freshly ground black pepper

Cranberry Gravy:

	Roast drippings
1	cup hot water
3	tablespoons all-purpose flour
1	teaspoon light brown sugar
⅛	teaspoon dried marjoram
⅛	teaspoon freshly ground black pepper
½	cup cranberry juice

1. Preheat the oven to 350°F. In a small bowl, combine the sugar, thyme, and pepper. Rub the mixture over the roast. Cover the ends with aluminum foil. Bake the roast in a large, shallow roasting pan with a rack for 1 hour.

2. Melt the butter in a small skillet over medium heat before adding the celery and onion. Sauté until the vegetables are tender.

3. Combine the bread cubes and broth in a large bowl, then stir in the rice, cranberries, parsley, brown sugar, Worcestershire sauce, poultry seasoning, pepper, and the cooked onions and celery.

4. Take the roast out of the oven and spoon the mixture into the center of it, being careful not to burn yourself. Continue roasting for 30 minutes more or until a meat thermometer reads 145°F.

5. Take the roast out of the oven and remove the foil from the ends. Lightly cover the roast and let it rest for 15 minutes. Move the stuffing to a serving dish and slice the roast between the ribs. Serve with Cranberry Gravy.

For the gravy:

1. Pour the pan drippings into a large, heat-safe measuring cup and skim the fat. Add enough hot water to bring the liquid to 1¼ cups.

2. In a small saucepan, combine the flour, brown sugar, marjoram, pepper, and cranberry juice. Gradually stir in the drippings. Bring the mixture to a boil, then continue cooking and stirring for 2 minutes or until the gravy thickens.

JOE'S HAM WITH PINEAPPLE

Serves 15

Enjoy while watching Christmas in Evergreen

2017 – Starring Ashley Williams as Allie Shaw and Teddy Sears as Ryan Bellamy, plus Malcolm Stewart as Joe

When you have a diner full of family and friends, old and new, gathering for a Christmas Feast, it makes sense to whip up more than one main dish. No need to make yourself crazy, though. Kringle Kitchen owner Joe makes a festively decorated baked ham that's as classic as Allie's red pickup truck.

1	(12-pound) bone-in ham
½	cup whole cloves
1	(20-ounce) can pineapple rings in heavy syrup
½	cup packed brown sugar
1	(20-ounce) bottle lemon-lime soda
1	(4-ounce) jar maraschino cherries

1. Preheat the oven to 325°F. Place the ham in a roasting pan. Score the rind of the ham in a diamond pattern, then press a clove into the center of each diamond.

2. In a large bowl, combine the juice from the pineapple rings, the brown sugar, and the lemon-lime soda. Pour this mixture over the whole surface of the ham.

3. Place the pineapple rings all over the ham in whatever arrangement you like. In the center of each ring, use a toothpick to secure a maraschino cherry.

4. Move the ham to the oven and bake it, uncovered, for 4–5 hours—basting frequently with its own juices—until a meat thermometer pushed into the meat (but not to the bone) reads 160°F. Remove the toothpicks before serving.

   Note: If your pineapple gets dark too quickly, loosely cover the ham with aluminum foil.

GRANDMA'S MEATBALLS

Serves 8-10

Enjoy while watching *The Christmas Ornament*

2013 – Starring Kellie Martin as Kathy Howard and Cameron Mathison as Tim Pierce

When you run a busy Christmas tree lot and gift shop, you need to keep up your strength—even if it means grabbing your meals (and meatballs) on the go. You could tell by the temptation on Tim's face how good Grandma's Meatballs are. So they're probably even better when served at the dinner table and covered in sauce.

⅔   cup Italian bread crumbs

     Milk to moisten bread crumbs

1   pound pork sausage

1   pound ground beef

½   cup grated Parmigiano-Reggiano cheese

2   large eggs

⅓   cup chopped fresh parsley

⅓   cup finely minced onions

3   cloves garlic, minced

1   teaspoon Italian seasoning

¼   teaspoon freshly ground black pepper

½   teaspoon kosher salt

1   tablespoon Worcestershire sauce

½   teaspoon garlic powder

1   tablespoon olive oil

1. In a large bowl, combine the bread crumbs and just enough milk to moisten them. Add the rest of the ingredients except the olive oil to the bowl and mix until just combined. (Overmixing will create denser meatballs.)

2. Preheat the oven to 375°F. Form the meatball mixture into 2-inch meatballs. Heat the olive oil in a large skillet over medium heat, then brown the meatballs in the skillet.

3. Place the browned meatballs on a baking sheet and bake them in the oven for 15–20 minutes. Top with your favorite sauce.

HOLIDAY MOJITO

*Enjoy while watching **A Dream of Christmas***

2016 – Starring Nikki Deloach as Penny and Andrew W. Walker as Stuart

Sometimes the best thing to do when you're confused (because you've jumped into an alternate timeline, gained a swanky promotion, and lost a devoted husband) is sit down, sip a festive and delicious drink, and take stock. It helps when the bartender knows exactly what you want, even if you don't.

Cranberry Syrup

8	ounces fresh cranberries
1	cup water
1	cup granulated sugar

Holiday Mojito

	Coarse sugar, for rimming the glass
20	fresh mint leaves
3	tablespoons lime juice
4	ounces Cranberry Syrup
4	ounces white rum
	Ice cubes
4	ounces sparkling water
	Fresh cranberries, for serving
	Fresh mint leaves, for serving

"I just want you to know that the world isn't going to come to an end if the tree lights are all wrong and if the gingerbread house topples."

—Ellen Gray, *Christmas List*

For the syrup:

1. Bring all of the syrup ingredients to a simmer in a small saucepan over medium heat. Reduce the heat to low and let the mixture continue to cook until the sugar has dissolved completely and the cranberries have softened and burst, about 10 minutes.

2. Allow the mixture to cool before straining it, pressing the cranberries against the strainer to expel as much liquid as possible. Discard the cranberries and refrigerate the syrup in an airtight container.

For the Holiday Mojito:

1. Moisten the rims of two glasses with water or extra lime juice, then dip them into a shallow plate of coarse sugar.

2. Divide the mint leaves and lime juice evenly between the glasses. Use a wooden spoon to press the mint leaves and muddle them in the juice. Stir 2 ounces of syrup and 2 ounces of white rum into each glass, then top them both with ice and 2 ounces of sparkling water. Garnish each with fresh cranberries and several mint leaves before serving.

CHRISTMAS PARTY PUNCH

Serves 20

Enjoy while watching *Once Upon a Holiday*

2015 – Starring Briana Evigan as Katie and Paul Campbell as Jack Langdon

Nothing helps you get to know a handsome stranger you've just met, plus several of his closest Santa-suit-wearing friends, like a cup of bright and fruity holiday punch—especially when it's spiked. What you learn might open your eyes and your heart.

---

1 large bag of ice

5 cups 100% juice cranberry beverage

2 bottles very dry sparkling wine

2 cups apple cider

1½ cups (1 can) diet ginger ale

1½ cups dark rum or brandy

2 oranges, thinly sliced in rounds

1 cup fresh cranberries

1. Pour the ice into a large punch bowl. Stir in the juice, wine, cider, ginger ale, and rum—all straight from the refrigerator.

2. Top the bowl or individual cups with orange slices and a smattering of fresh cranberries before serving.

MISTLETOE FIZZ

Serves 2

Enjoy while watching *The Christmas Train*

2017 – Starring Dermot Mulroney as Tom Langdon, Kimberly Williams-Paisley as Eleanor Carter,
and Danny Glover as Max Powers

If you're hanging out under the mistletoe, waiting for an old flame to join you, the Mistletoe Fizz is the drink for you. As bartender Kenny says, "Drink one and you'll kiss the one you love." Sometimes fate needs a helping hand (or twelve), so take a deep breath and share this joyful drink with that special someone.

Rosemary Syrup

¼	cup fresh rosemary leaves
1	cup water
1	cup granulated sugar

Mistletoe Fizz

4	ounces gin
2	ounces cranberry juice
1	ounce Rosemary Syrup
	Prosecco, to fill
6	fresh cranberries, for serving
2	sprigs rosemary, for serving

For the syrup:

1. Combine all ingredients in a small saucepan and bring the mixture to a boil. Continue cooking until the sugar dissolves, then let the mixture simmer for 1 minute more.

2. Remove the pan from the heat and let the syrup steep for 30 minutes before straining it. Keep the syrup refrigerated in an airtight container.

For the Mistletoe Fizz:

1. Add the gin, cranberry juice, and Rosemary Syrup to a shaker with ice. Shake it and strain the mixture into two ice-filled glasses.

2. Fill the rest of each glass with Prosecco. Top both drinks off with fresh cranberries skewered on a sprig of rosemary.

GINGERBREAD MARTINI

Serves 4

Enjoy while watching *A Gingerbread Romance*

2018 – Starring Tia Mowry-Hardrict as Taylor Scott and Duane Henry as Adam Dale

The Gingerbread Martini is a lot easier to make than an architecturally perfect, life-size gingerbread house. And since gingerbread brought them together, Taylor and Adam can use this cozy cocktail to toast their happy ending in Philadelphia.

Gingerbread Syrup

1	cup granulated sugar
1	cup water
5	whole cloves
2	cinnamon sticks
1	(2-inch) piece fresh ginger, cut into rounds

Gingerbread Martini

4	ounces Irish cream liqueur
4	ounces vodka
2	ounces coffee liqueur
2	ounces Gingerbread Syrup
2	scoops vanilla ice cream, softened
	Ice cubes
	Whipped cream, for serving
	Gingerbread cookies, crushed, for serving

For the syrup:

1. Add all of the syrup ingredients to a small saucepan over medium-high heat and bring them to a boil. Once the sugar has dissolved, reduce the heat to low and let the mixture simmer for 5 minutes.

2. Remove the syrup from the heat and let it cool before straining it. Refrigerate it in an airtight container for up 2 weeks.

For the Gingerbread Martini:

1. Add the Irish cream liqueur, vodka, coffee liqueur, Gingerbread Syrup, and ice cream to a cocktail shaker.

2. Add the ice and shake well before pouring the cocktail into four martini glasses. Top each with whipped cream and cookie crumbs.

THE DE VICO COMET

Serves 1

Enjoy while watching *Journey Back to Christmas*

2016 – Starring Candace Cameron Bure as Hanna and Oliver Hudson as Jake

This alcoholic drink is just as sweet, fiery, and memorable as nurse Hanna herself. When set aflame, it dazzles like the de Vico comet. And depending on how many of these you have, you might just feel like you've been sent traveling through time, too.

1¼	ounces butterscotch schnapps
1¼	ounces Irish cream liqueur
1¼	ounces cinnamon schnapps
	Float sambuca
1	pinch cinnamon or nutmeg

1. In a cocktail shaker filled with ice, combine the butterscotch schnapps, Irish cream liqueur, and cinnamon schnapps. Strain the mixture into a cocktail glass.

2. Float the sambuca, then top the drink with a dusting of cinnamon or nutmeg. Just before serving, flame the drink.

HOLIDAY-STYLE HOT TODDY

Serves 4
Enjoy while watching your favorite Christmas movie

Cozy up with a cup of this holiday staple when you're ready to play the famous cozy Christmas Movie Drinking Game. The rules are simple: take a sip whenever you see a cozy Christmas–movie cliché. City person moves to a small town? Sip. Character's name is Christmas inspired? Sip. Santa plays matchmaker? You get the idea! (Drink responsibly!)

4	cups apple cider
1	large orange, sliced
½	cup fresh cranberries, plus more for serving
3	sprigs of rosemary
1	teaspoon ground cinnamon
4	(1½-ounce) shots cinnamon whiskey
4	orange slices, for serving

1. Add the apple cider, sliced orange, cranberries, rosemary, and cinnamon to a large pot over high heat and bring the mixture to a boil.

2. Reduce the heat to low and let the mixture simmer, uncovered, until the cranberries begin to soften, about 10–20 minutes.

3. Prepare four heat-safe glasses with 1 shot each of the whiskey. Add 1 cup of the cider mixture to each glass. Garnish each with fresh cranberries and an orange slice, and serve them hot.

THE DIVA

Serves 1

Enjoy while watching *A Christmas Melody*

2015 – Starring Lacey Chabert as Kristin Parson, Brennan Elliott as Danny Collier,
and Mariah Carey as Melissa McKean-Atkinson

Someone get Kristin a cocktail! Lacey Chabert is used to dealing with mean girls, but Mariah Carey takes the diva role to a whole new level. Melissa McKean-Atkinson may have a dentist husband, 3 children, and a huge 4-bedroom, 3½-bath, 2-story house, but she obviously does not have the Christmas spirit.

2	dashes cranberry bitters
½	ounce simple syrup
½	ounce orange liqueur
1½	ounces fresh grapefruit juice
1½	ounces Mezcal Vago
	Ice
	Lemon peel, for garnish

1. Combine all of the drink ingredients and the ice in a shaker, shake well, and strain the cocktail into a martini glass. Garnish with a twist of lemon peel.

CHAPTER 3:
SWEET TREATS

CRAZY-FOR-MERINGUE CHRISTMAS TREES

Yield: 24 trees

Enjoy while watching *Fir Crazy*

2013 – Starring Sarah Lancaster as Elise MacReynolds and Eric Johnson as Darren Foster

Once you learn to appreciate the magic of Christmas, you can't help but find new ways to celebrate it—like upgrading your boring black coffee to a Yule Log Latte. Join Elise in hugging the holiday spirit with these sweet little tree-shaped confections, which are perfect for both enticing tree-lot customers and bribing a class full of fifth-graders to like you.

	Nonstick cooking spray
4	egg whites
1	cup granulated sugar
½	teaspoon of cream of tartar
1	tablespoon butter-vanilla bakery emulsion
	Green food coloring
	Large gold or star sprinkles, for tree toppers
	Red and green sprinkles

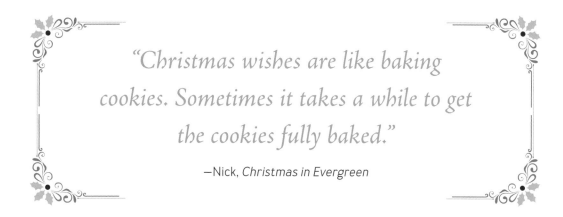

"Christmas wishes are like baking cookies. Sometimes it takes a while to get the cookies fully baked."

—Nick, *Christmas in Evergreen*

1. Preheat the oven to 225°F. Line a large baking sheet with aluminum foil sprayed lightly with cooking spray.

2. Using a hand or stand mixer on high, whip the egg whites for several minutes until they become frothy. Very gradually mix in the sugar, then mix for 1 minute more.

3. Add the cream of tartar, butter-vanilla emulsion, and food coloring, and continue to mix on high until stiff peaks form.

   Note: Add the food coloring one or two drops at a time until you reach the desired shade of green for your Christmas trees.

4. Gently spoon the meringue into an icing bag with a star-shaped frosting tip. Slowly swirl the meringue onto the foil, starting with larger circles at the base (about 2 inches across) and working your way into smaller circles until you reach the top, forming your mini Christmas trees. (Picture soft-serve swirled onto a cone.)

5. Top each tree with a gold ball, star, or other tree topper and sprinkle your red and green "decorations" over the rest of the tree. (You can decorate your trees in whatever colors you like.)

6. Bake the meringues for 45 minutes or until you notice them browning just at the edges. Let them cool completely before serving or storing in an airtight container.

CHARLIE'S CUT-OUT CHRISTMAS COOKIES

——— Yield: 24–48 cookies ———
Enjoy while watching *A Shoe Addict's Christmas*

2018 – Starring Candace Cameron Bure as Noelle Carpenter, Luke Macfarlane
as Jake Marsden, and Jean Smart as Charlie

Santa's angels know there's nothing like planning a Christmas party or baking cookies to bring two fated lovebirds together. As Charlie says, Christmas cookies "taste so much better when you make them yourself, with love!" The number of cookies you get from the recipe depends on the sizes and shapes you choose. (Bonus points for using a shoe-shaped cookie cutter!)

Cookies

1	cup unsalted butter
1	cup powdered sugar
1	large egg, beaten
1½	teaspoons almond extract
1	teaspoon pure vanilla extract
1	teaspoon kosher salt
2½	cups all-purpose flour, sifted
	Nonstick cooking spray

Royal Icing

4	cups powdered sugar, sifted
2	tablespoons meringue powder
5	tablespoons cold water

For the cookies:

1. Preheat the oven to 375°F. Use an electric mixer with a paddle attachment to cream the butter on low speed. Mix in the powdered sugar until well combined, then blend in the egg, almond extract, vanilla, salt, and flour until the dough forms.

2. Put the dough in the refrigerator to chill until firm. Then roll it out on a well-floured surface until it's ¼ inch thick. Use cookie cutters to create your shapes and place them on lightly greased baking sheets.

3. Bake your cookies (placed 2 inches apart) for 8–10 minutes, being careful not to let them brown. Allow them to cool before frosting them. If the included instructions for Royal Icing seem too complicated, feel free to use prepackaged icing!

For the Royal Icing:

1. Using the electric mixer with the paddle attachment, mix together all of the icing ingredients on low for 8–10 minutes until the icing has a matte finish. The icing will be stiff, so mix in water just a tablespoon at a time until the icing loosens to a consistency you can pipe neat lines with.

   Note: If you want to use multiple colors, separate the icing into small airtight containers and stir the desired food coloring into each. Keep the icing sealed in the containers until you're ready to use it so it doesn't dry out. You could also use white icing and decorate with colorful sprinkles.

2. To create neatly iced cookies, spoon some of the icing into a piping bag and use it to outline your shapes. Keep the rest of the icing in an airtight container while you let the outlines set. When you're ready, stir a small amount of water into the remaining icing, and spoon this thinner icing onto your cookies to fill in your outline. Allow the icing to set before enjoying your cookies.

AUNT SALLY'S SANTA SHORTBREADS

—— Yield: 12–24 shortbreads ——
Enjoy while watching _Christmas Cookies_

2016 – Starring Jill Wagner as Hannah Harper and Wes Brown as Jake Carter

When you set up shop in a town called Cookie Jar, you have to have a really great Christmas cookie recipe, and Aunt Sally's Cookie Company doesn't disappoint. These Santa shortbreads are her signature (and super-secret) recipe—one known to change workaholic Grinches into small-town-saving heroes. Just remember the secret ingredient: love!

Cookies

1   cup salted butter, cold and cut into pieces

½   cup granulated sugar

1   teaspoon vanilla extract or almond extract

2¼   cups all-purpose flour

Icing

1   cup powdered sugar

2   teaspoons milk

2   teaspoons light corn syrup

¼   teaspoon almond extract
       Food coloring

For the cookies:

1. Using an electric mixer on low speed, cream together the butter, sugar, and vanilla until well combined. Add the flour and continue mixing to form the dough.

2. Knead the dough by hand for 5 minutes until it is soft and pliable but not sticky. Roll it up into a ball, wrap it in plastic wrap, and let it chill in the refrigerator for 30 minutes.

3. Preheat the oven to 350°F and line your baking sheets with parchment paper. Once the dough has chilled, roll it out on a lightly floured surface until it's ¼ inch thick. Use a Santa-shaped cookie cutter to make your cookies.

4. Place the cookies (2 inches apart) onto lined baking sheets, and bake them for 8–10 minutes or until the edges are golden brown. Immediately move them to a wire rack to cool.

For the icing:

1. Stir together the sugar and milk in a small bowl until smooth, then mix in the corn syrup and almond extract. The icing should be smooth and glossy. Add more powdered sugar to thicken it or more corn syrup to thin it out.

   Note: For multiple colors, divide the icing into separate bowls and add the desired food coloring. For Santa Shortbreads, you would color some red for his hat and leave some white for his beard and the hat's fur lining.

2. Spoon the icing into a piping bag and pipe it onto the cookies, or use a brush or spoon to decorate the cookies with it.

KYLIE'S GINGERBREAD STARS

Yield: 28 stars

*Enjoy while watching **The Sweetest Christmas***

2017 – Starring Lacey Chabert as Kylie Watson and Lea Coco as Nick Mazzanti

When you're trying to bake and decorate an elaborate gingerbread creation, you need all of the focus you can muster. If you have to distract two adorable nieces with gingerbread cookies, so be it! These sweet gingerbread stars will not only keep them from picking at your contest entry, they'll also make them feel included in the fun.

1	cup packed light brown sugar
¾	cup unsalted butter, softened
½	cup molasses
1	large egg
3	cups all-purpose flour
2	teaspoons ground ginger
2	teaspoons ground cinnamon
1	teaspoon baking soda

½	teaspoon kosher salt
½	teaspoon ground cloves
	Nonstick cooking spray
4	ounces white chocolate baking bars or squares, chopped
2	tablespoons coarse white sparkling sugar

"I have to show him how I feel in the best way I know how: with gingerbread."

—Kylie Watson, *The Sweetest Christmas*

1. Add the brown sugar, butter, molasses, and egg to a large bowl and use an electric mixer on medium speed to beat them together until they're well combined. Switch the speed to low before mixing in the flour, ginger, cinnamon, baking soda, salt, and cloves.

2. Roll the dough into a ball on a lightly floured surface, then flatten it into a disc. Wrap the dough in plastic wrap and let it chill in the refrigerator until firm, about 1 hour.

3. Preheat the oven to 350°F and lightly grease large cookie sheets. Remove the dough from the refrigerator and roll it out on a lightly floured surface until it's ¼ inch thick. Use a 3- or 4-inch star-shaped cookie cutter to make your cookies.

4. Bake the cookies (placed 2 inches apart) for 10–12 minutes or until stiff to the touch in the center. Move them to a cooling rack to cool completely before decorating.

5. Melt the white chocolate uncovered in the microwave on high power, about 45 seconds to 1 minute. Stir it until it's smooth and drizzle or pipe it over the cookies in an abstract pattern. Sprinkle the chocolate with the sparkling sugar before it sets, and let the finished cookies stand for 30 minutes before serving or storing in an airtight container.

OATMEAL SNOWFLAKES

Yield: 60–72 cookies

Enjoy while watching *A Christmas Melody*

2015 – Starring Lacey Chabert as Kristin Parson, Brennan Elliott as Danny Collier,
and Mariah Carey as Melissa McKean-Atkinson

There's nothing like the magic of a first snowfall—especially when it's your first in years. For Kristin, it feels like a sign that she made the right choice in moving her daughter, Emily, from temperate LA to her wintery hometown of Silver Falls. These crispy oatmeal cookies inspire that same joy in every bite!

1	cup old-fashioned oats
1	cup granulated sugar
2	tablespoons + 1 teaspoon all-purpose flour
½	teaspoon kosher salt
1	stick unsalted butter, melted and cooled
1	large egg, beaten
2	teaspoons almond extract

1. Preheat the oven to 350°F. In a large bowl, combine all of the dry ingredients. Stir in the wet ingredients until well combined. (If the batter seems thin, you can add more oatmeal.)

2. Line a baking sheet with aluminum foil and drop the batter in half teaspoons, leaving 2 inches between them for spreading.

3. Bake the cookies for 8–10 minutes per batch until they are lightly browned. Allow them to cool for 1–2 minutes, then peel them off the aluminum foil.

SNOW BALL COOKIES

Yield: 72 cookies

Enjoy while watching Christmas Wonderland

2018 – Starring Emily Osment as Heidi Nelson and Ryan Rottman as Chris Shepherd

Throwing a middle-school dance is no small feat, especially when the school gym floods and you're forced to find a new location. But as these high-school sweethearts discover, a detour can be exactly what you need. (If you have Heidi's baking skills, you might want to stick to decorating and skip contributing to the refreshments.)

2	sticks unsalted butter, softened
5	tablespoons granulated sugar
2	teaspoons pure vanilla extract
¼	teaspoon kosher salt
2	cups all-purpose flour
2	cups finely chopped walnuts
1½	cups powdered sugar

1. In a large bowl, cream the butter and sugar with an electric mixer. Mix in the vanilla and salt, then slowly beat in the flour a little at a time. Stir in the nuts. Divide the dough in two, wrapping each half in plastic wrap and refrigerating them both for 45 minutes.

2. Place the rack in the middle of the oven and preheat it to 350°F. Pour the powdered sugar into a small bowl. Roll the dough into 1-inch balls.

3. Place your snowballs on lined baking sheets, leaving 1–2 inches between them for expansion. Let them bake for 12–14 minutes until the cookies are just beginning to brown.

4. Move baked cookies to a cooling rack for 2 minutes, then gently roll the still-warm snowballs in powdered sugar to coat. Let them cool completely on the wire rack before rolling them a second time in the sugar. Store the finished snowballs in an airtight container for up to 4 weeks.

CINNAMON TEA COOKIES

Yield: 30 cookies

Enjoy while watching *Once Upon a Holiday*

2015 – Starring Briana Evigan as Katie Hollingston and Paul Campbell as Jack Langdon

George knows exactly how to calm the royals of Montsauri—a cup of tea and a willing ear. Adding some scrumptious cinnamon cookies to his impromptu therapy sessions could only help. Even rebellious European princesses with American accents enjoy tea time and a sugary treat when their stress levels are rising.

1⅓ cups all-purpose flour

¾ teaspoon ground cinnamon

¼ teaspoon kosher salt

¼ teaspoon baking soda

10 tablespoons unsalted butter, softened

1 cup granulated sugar

1 large egg

1 teaspoon pure vanilla extract

1. Preheat the oven to 375°F and line a baking sheet or two with parchment paper.

2. In a small bowl, sift together the flour, cinnamon, salt, and baking soda. In a large bowl, use an electric mixture on low to cream together the butter and sugar, then mix in the egg and vanilla extract. Stir the dry mixture into the wet one to create the dough.

3. Scoop and roll the dough into 1-inch balls and place them about 2 inches apart on the lined baking sheets.

4. Let the cookies bake for 12–15 minutes or until they are lightly browned. Let the finished cookies cool before storing them in an airtight container for up to 2 weeks.

AUNT RUBY'S CHOCOLATE CHIP COOKIES

Yield: 24 cookies

Enjoy while watching *Christmas Joy*

2018 – Starring Danielle Panabaker as Joy Holbrook and Matt Long as Ben Andrews,
plus Beverley Elliott as Aunt Ruby

Aunt Ruby doesn't mess around when it comes to the Crystal Falls Cookie Crawl. Among the dozens of cookies that her niece, Joy, is now responsible for making, classic chocolate chip seems to be the favorite. If you're prepping the dough ahead of time, just make sure that the door to the fridge is fully closed before you walk away!

1	cup salted butter, softened
½	cup granulated sugar
1½	cups packed brown sugar
2	large eggs, room temperature
2	teaspoons pure vanilla extract
1	teaspoon baking soda
2	teaspoons hot water
½	teaspoon kosher salt
3	cups all-purpose flour
2	cups semisweet chocolate chips
1	cup chopped walnuts (optional)

1. Preheat the oven to 350°F and line two baking sheets with parchment paper.

2. Add the butter and sugars to a large bowl, and use an electric mixer on low to cream them together. Mix in the eggs one at a time, then mix in the vanilla.

3. Combine the baking soda and hot water in a small bowl, then add it and the salt to the batter. Using a spatula, stir in the flour, chocolate chips, and walnuts (optional) until well combined.

4. Scoop and roll the dough into 1-inch balls and place them about 2 inches apart.

5. Bake the cookies for about 10 minutes until they just begin to brown (they may look underdone), Let them cool before serving or storing them in an airtight container. cooling rack and then storing them in an airtight container.

STOLEN CHOCOLATE COOKIE TRUFFLES

Yield: 24 truffles
Enjoy while watching *Window Wonderland*

2013 – Starring Chyler Leigh as Sloan Van Doren and Paul Campbell as Jake Dooley

It's not really stealing if your boss was supposed to share that big basket of goodies with you, but sneaking a few these chocolate truffles in the middle of the night might just make them taste better. One thing is for sure—Mr. Fitch is getting a lump of coal in his stocking, along with some makeup remover for that silly fake mustache.

---

1 (16-ounce) package chocolate sandwich cookies, divided

1 (8-ounce) package cream cheese, softened

2 (8-ounce) packages semisweet baking chocolate

1. Using a food processor, crumble 9 of the sandwich cookies. Reserve this for later use. In the same food processor, crumble the rest of the cookies into fine crumbs and pour them into a medium bowl.

2. Stir the cream cheese into the cookie crumbles until well combined. Roll this mixture into 42 balls, each about 1 inch in diameter.

3. Use a double-boiler to melt the chocolate and keep it warm while you dip the balls to cover them.

   Note: Chilling the majority of the cookie balls in the refrigerator while you dip a few at a time can help them keep their shape.

4. Move dipped truffles to a baking sheet lined with wax paper and sprinkle them with the reserved cookie crumbles before they set.

5. Move finished truffles to the refrigerator to firm up for 1 hour. Store any uneaten truffles covered and in the refrigerator.

PEPPERMINT HOT CHOCOLATE COOKIES

Yield: 42 cookies

Enjoy while watching **Christmas in Evergreen: Letters to Santa**

2018 – Starring Jill Wagner as Lisa and Mark Deklin as Kevin

When faced with a charmingly decorated hot cocoa cart in the town square, don't be the guy that orders a black coffee. Follow Lisa's lead and go for the peppermint hot chocolate—with extra whipped cream, of course. And if you can't get to the cocoa cart, whip up these festive cookies instead. 'Tis the season, Kevin.

1   cup unsalted butter, softened

1   cup granulated sugar

1   large egg

1   teaspoon peppermint extract

2 ⅓   cups all-purpose flour

⅓   cup baking cocoa

1   teaspoon kosher salt

1   teaspoon baking soda

1   (11½-ounce) package milk chocolate chips

1   cup marshmallow creme

1   cup finely crushed peppermint candy

1. Preheat the oven to 375°F and line two baking sheets with parchment paper. Add the butter and sugar to a large bowl, and use an electric mixer on low to cream them together. Beat in the egg and peppermint extract.

2. In another large bowl, stir together the flour, baking cocoa, salt, and baking soda. Add the dry mixture to the wet one and mix well.

3. Drop the dough by the tablespoon onto your lined baking sheets. Let the cookies bake for 10–12 minutes until the tops crack, then move them to wire racks to cool completely.

4. Microwave the chocolate chips for 30 seconds at a time, stirring in between, until the chocolate is melted and smooth. Top each cookie with a dollop of marshmallow creme and a dollop of melted chocolate, then immediately sprinkle each with crushed peppermint candy. Let the cookies stand until set, then store them in an airtight container.

MELANIE'S VANILLA BEAN SUGAR COOKIES

——— Yield: 24 cookies ———
Enjoy while watching *Matchmaker Santa*

2012 – Starring Lacey Chabert as Melanie Hogan and Adam Mayfield as Dean Ford,
plus Florence Henderson as Peggy and Lin Shaye as Debbie

Melanie's secret to the perfect Christmas cookies: pure vanilla bean extract. Santa's secret to helping people find their soulmates: stranding them with people who are not their current significant others. Either way, everything seems to work out wonderfully!

———

3	cups all-purpose flour
2	teaspoons baking powder
2	sticks unsalted butter, cut into chunks
1	cup vanilla sugar
1	large egg
3/4	teaspoon pure vanilla extract
1/2	teaspoon pure almond extract
1	vanilla bean, scraped (optional)
	Favorite icing and sprinkles (optional)

1. Preheat the oven to 350°F and line two baking sheets with parchment paper. In a medium bowl, stir together the flour and baking powder.

2. Add the butter and sugar to a large bowl, and use an electric mixer on low to cream them together. Stir in the egg, extracts, and vanilla seeds (optional) before slowly incorporating the flour mixture.

3. On a lightly floured surface, roll the dough out until it's ¼ inch thick. Use your favorite cookie cutters to make the cookies and spread them out over the lined baking sheets.

4. Move the baking sheets to the freezer for 5–7 minutes, then to the oven for 10–12 minutes until the cookies just begin to brown.

5. Let the cookies rest on the baking sheets for 3 minutes before moving them to a cooling rack to cool completely. Serve them plain, or decorate them with icing and sprinkles.

CHRISTMAS GRINCH CRACKLE COOKIES

Yield: 24 cookies
Enjoy while watching *Finding Christmas*

2017 – Starring Eric Winter as Ben White and Jodie Sweetin as Grace Long

Every cozy Christmas movie has its Grinch, and he or she is usually too busy to bake anything (hence the boxed cake mix in this recipe). Ben, for example, can't possibly take time away from his writing to bring joy to his hometown and pride to his Santa-suit-wearing father. But the trappings of Christmas win every time, and Ben's heart grew three sizes the year he met Grace.

1   [15¼-ounce] box vanilla cake mix

½   cup unsalted butter, softened

2   large eggs

1   tablespoon oil

    Green food coloring

½   cup powdered sugar

½   cup cornstarch

    Green decorating gel or frosting

24   red heart sprinkles

1. Preheat the oven to 375°F and line a baking sheet with parchment paper.

2. In a large mixing bowl, stir together the dry cake mix with the butter, eggs, and oil until well combined. Add the green food coloring a drop or two at a time until the dough reaches the color of green you want.

3. Scoop and roll the dough into 1-inch balls. In a small bowl, combine the powdered sugar and cornstarch. Roll the cookie balls through the powdered-sugar mixture and place them 1–2 inches apart on the lined baking sheet.

4. Bake the cookies for 8–10 minutes until they crack, being careful not to let them brown. Remove them from the oven and let them sit for 2 minutes on the baking sheet before moving them to a cooling rack to finish cooling.

5. Use a small dot of green decorating gel to adhere a candy heart to each cookie.

MOLLY'S PEPPERMINT-MOCHA COOKIES

Yield: 18 cookies

Enjoy while watching *Mingle All the Way*

2018 – Starring Jen Lilley as Molly Hoffman and Brant Daugherty as Jeff Scanlon

Molly's app may have been inspired by the holiday season, but it definitely doesn't capture the spirit of it. Soon enough, though, the true meaning of Christmas catches up with her and she finds herself infusing her days with all things merry. So whether it's love or just the Christmas spirit that moves you, upgrade your coffee order and your cookies this holiday season.

¾	cup Dutch-process cocoa powder
2	cups all-purpose flour
2	teaspoons espresso powder
1	teaspoon baking powder
½	teaspoon kosher salt
1	cup shortening
1¾	cups packed light brown sugar
2	large eggs, room temperature
1	teaspoon peppermint extract
2	tablespoons whole milk
3½	ounces semisweet chocolate, melted and slightly cooled
8	ounces white chocolate, finely chopped
4	full-size candy canes, finely chopped

1. Preheat the oven to 350°F and line two baking sheets with parchment paper. In a large bowl, whisk together the cocoa powder, flour, espresso powder, baking powder, and salt until well combined. Set this aside.

2. Add the shortening and brown sugar to a separate large bowl, and use an electric mixture on medium to combine them until light and fluffy—scraping down the sides when necessary—about 3 minutes. Mix in the eggs, peppermint extract, and milk.

3. Reduce the speed to low and gradually combine the dry mixture with the wet one. Stir in the melted chocolate until just combined.

4. Scoop the dough by the ¼ cup and place the cookies 2 inches apart on the lined baking sheets. (Use a spatula to remove the sticky dough from the measuring cup.)

5. Bake the cookies one sheet at a time for 9–10 minutes until the edges have set and the tops are slightly puffed. Move baked cookies to a wire rack to cool completely, about 30 minutes. Keep the lined baking sheets handy.

6. Add the white chocolate to a microwaveable bowl. Microwave it for 30 seconds at a time, stirring in between, until the chocolate is melted and smooth. Dip each cookie in the melted chocolate before sprinkling it with crushed candy cane. Let the cookies set on the lined baking sheets, about 1 hour, before storing them in an airtight container for up to 2 days.

McDOUGAL'S EGGNOG MACARONS

Yield: 30 macarons

Enjoy while watching My Christmas Dream

2016 – Starring Danica McKellar as Christina and David Haydn-Jones as Kurt

McDougal's department store is going international, and Danica McKellar's Christina can't think of anything better than managing the new Paris store. But if she finds her love locally and decides to stay in town, she might need to settle for some homemade macarons. Lucky for her, these Eggnog Macarons are exquisite!

Macarons

- 2 cups powdered sugar
- 1 cup almond flour
- ¼ teaspoon ground cinnamon
- ¼ teaspoon ground cloves
- ¼ teaspoon ground nutmeg
- 3 egg whites
- ¼ cup granulated sugar
- ¼ teaspoon cream of tartar
- Pinch kosher salt

Filling

- 1 cup powdered sugar
- ¼ teaspoon ground cinnamon
- ¼ teaspoon ground nutmeg
- ⅛ teaspoon ground cloves
- ½ cup unsalted butter, softened
- 1 teaspoon pure vanilla extract
- 1 tablespoon brandy

For the macarons:

1. Preheat the oven to 350°F and line two baking sheets with parchment paper. Sift the powdered sugar, almond flour, and spices into a large bowl, discarding anything left in the sifter.

2. In another large bowl, use an electric mixer on medium to beat the egg whites, granulated sugar, cream of tartar, and salt until foamy. Continue beating the batter on high speed for 5 minutes until medium peaks form.

3. Gently fold in the flour mixture ⅓ at a time, frequently scraping the bottom and sides of the bowl. Spoon the batter into a pastry bag fitted with a ½-inch round tip. Pipe 1½-inch circles about 2 inches apart onto the lined baking sheets.

4. Bake one sheet at a time for 11–12 minutes or until the macarons are set. Place the baking sheet on a wire rack and let the macarons cool completely before removing them from the parchment paper.

For the filling:

1. Combine the sugar and spices in a small bowl. Add the butter and vanilla to a large bowl, and use an electric mixer on medium to beat them together. Gradually beat in the sugar mixture, frequently scraping the bottom and sides of the bowl.

2. Beat in the brandy until the batter is smooth, then spoon it into a piping bag fitted with a small round tip. Assemble the macarons by piping the filling onto the flat side of 1 cookie and sandwiching it with another cookie. Repeat with the remaining cookies, and store the finished macarons in the refrigerator in an airtight container for up to 7 days.

BAKED GARLAND, ALASKA

Serves 16

Enjoy while watching *Christmas Under Wraps*

2014 – Starring Candace Cameron Bure as Dr. Lauren Brunell and David O'Donnell as Andy Holliday

Dr. Lauren Brunell learns the hard way that it's a long way to Alaska, and there's a lot of work to be done for the only local doctor. But that's Garland for ya! If you're looking for a shortcut, there's no harm in using a boxed brownie mix to create this magical dessert.

Ice Cream Dome

6	cups peppermint ice cream, softened
10	cups vanilla ice cream, softened

Brownie Base

	Nonstick cooking spray
1	cup unsalted butter
8	ounces bittersweet chocolate
4	large eggs
2	cups granulated sugar
2	teaspoons pure vanilla extract
1 ¼	cup all-purpose flour
1	teaspoon baking powder
½	teaspoon kosher salt

Meringue

8	egg whites, room temperature
¼	teaspoon cream of tartar
1	cup granulated sugar

For the ice cream:

1. Line a bowl with a 9-inch diameter (to match the brownie pan) with plastic wrap. Spread the peppermint ice cream into the bottom of the bowl, then layer in the vanilla ice cream. Cover the bowl with plastic wrap and freeze the ice cream until it's hard, preferably overnight.

For the brownie base:

1. Preheat the oven to 350°F. Grease a 9-inch cake pan with cooking spray, then line the bottom of the pan with parchment paper and spray the paper with more cooking spray.

2. Add the butter and chocolate to a microwaveable bowl. Microwave them for 30 seconds at a time, stirring in between, until they're melted, combined, and smooth. Set the bowl aside to cool.

3. In a large bowl, whisk together the eggs, sugar, and vanilla until well combined. In another large bowl, whisk together the flour, baking powder, and salt. Stir the chocolate mixture into the egg mixture, then stir the flour mixture into that until everything is well combined.

4. Pour the brownie batter into the cake pan and bake it for 50–60 minutes until a toothpick inserted in the center comes out clean.

5. Let the brownie base cool completely, about 1 hour, before turning it out onto a large, ovenproof serving plate. Top the brownie base with the frozen ice cream mound, cover it with plastic wrap, and put it back in the freezer.

For the meringue:

1. Using an electric mixer with a whisk attachment, beat the egg whites and cream of tartar on medium-high speed for 2 minutes. Increase the speed to high, then slowly whisk in the sugar until stiff, glossy peaks form.

To assemble the Baked Garland, Alaska:

1. Remove the center from the freezer, unwrap it, and cover the dome completely with meringue. Use a spoon to create swirls all over the meringue. Put the whole thing back in the freezer for at least 3 hours or up to 2 days.

2. When you're ready to serve it, put the cake in the oven at 500°F for 3–5 minutes or until the swirls begin to brown. Let it stand for 30 minutes before slicing and serving it.

MELTED SNOWMAN CUPCAKES

Yield: 12–14 cupcakes

Enjoy while watching *The Sweetest Christmas*

2017 – Starring Lacey Chabert as Kylie Watson and Lea Coco as Nick Mazzanti, plus Brenden Sunderland as Bobby

A recipe gone wrong doesn't have to be a disaster, especially when you have a trained baker handy. Kylie turns Bobby's lack of patience into this charming dessert without giving it a second thought. All it takes is a few marshmallows and some creative icing work.

Chocolate Cupcakes

¾	cup all-purpose flour
½	cup unsweetened natural cocoa powder
¾	teaspoon baking powder
½	teaspoon baking soda
¼	teaspoon kosher salt
2	large eggs, room temperature
½	cup granulated sugar
½	cup packed light brown sugar
⅓	cup vegetable or canola oil
2	teaspoons pure vanilla extract
½	cup buttermilk, room temperature

Marshmallow Frosting

1	cup granulated sugar
3	tablespoons water
2	large egg whites, room temperature
1	pinch cream of tartar
1	pinch kosher salt
12–14	marshmallows
	Black gel icing
	Orange gel icing

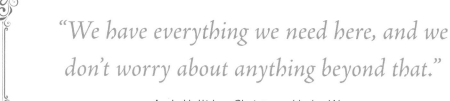

"We have everything we need here, and we don't worry about anything beyond that."

—Andy Holliday, *Christmas Under Wraps*

For the cupcakes:

1. Preheat the oven to 350°F and prepare a muffin pan with cupcake liners. In a large bowl, whisk together the flour, cocoa powder, baking powder, baking soda, and salt. In another large bowl, whisk together the eggs, sugars, oil, and vanilla until smooth. Gently combine the two mixtures, whisking in the buttermilk at the same time to create a thin batter. (Don't overmix it.)

2. Fill the liners with batter just to halfway. Bake the cupcakes for 18–21 minutes or until a toothpick inserted in the center of them comes out clean. Let the cupcakes cool while you make the frosting.

For the frosting:

1. Stir together the granulated sugar and water in a small saucepan and bring it to a boil over medium-high heat, stirring until the sugar dissolves, about 2–3 minutes.

2. Using an electric mixer on low, beat together the egg whites, cream of tartar, and salt until soft peaks form. Increase the speed to medium and continue mixing while pouring the hot sugar syrup into the egg whites. Continue mixing until the frosting becomes marshmallowy, about 5 minutes.

To assemble the Melted Snowman Cupcakes:

1. Top each cupcake with frosting and a marshmallow. Use the black icing to create each melted snowman's face, arms, and buttons and the orange icing to create the nose.

PRINCIPAL SUMNER'S PEPPERMINT SUGAR COOKIES

———— Yield: 30 cookies ————

Enjoy while watching *Switched for Christmas*

2017 – Starring Candace Cameron Bure as Kate Lockhart and Chris Dixon, Eion Bailey as Tom Kinder, and Mark Deklin as Greg Turner, plus James Jamison as Principal Sumner

The right cookie can go a long way when you're sweet-talking your boss into seeing things from your perspective. And Kate Lockhart knows exactly which one to use: a brightly flavored sugar cookie drizzled in white chocolate. Principle Sumner couldn't resist. Could you?

———————

2¾ cups all-purpose flour	1 large egg yolk
1 teaspoon baking soda	1 teaspoon pure vanilla extract
½ teaspoon kosher salt	¾ teaspoon peppermint extract
½ teaspoon cream of tartar	2½ cups (15 ounces) white baking chocolate, melted
1½ cups granulated sugar	Red and green icing in ready-to-use tubes
1 cup unsalted butter, softened	
1 large egg	

1. Preheat the oven to 350°F and line a baking sheet with parchment paper. In a large bowl, whisk together the flour, baking soda, salt, and cream of tartar. Set this mixture aside.

2. In another large bowl, use an electric mixer on low speed to cream together the sugar and butter, then mix in the egg, egg yolk, vanilla, and peppermint. Stir the dry mixture into the wet one until just combined to create the dough.

3. Scoop the dough, about 1½ tablespoons at a time, and shape it into balls. Transfer the balls to the prepared baking sheet so that they sit 2 inches apart. Chill the remaining dough until you're ready to scoop and bake it.

4. Bake the cookies for 10–11 minutes. They should appear slightly under-baked when you remove them from the oven. Let the cookies rest for several minutes on the hot baking sheet before transferring them to a wire rack to cool.

5. Cover another baking sheet or a flat surface with wax paper. Move the cooled cookies to the wax paper and use a spoon to lightly drizzle the white chocolate over them. For a more festive look, use the icing pens to decorate each cookie with a sprig of holly and berries. Once the chocolate has set completely, store the cookies in an airtight container at room temperature.

HAPPY GINGERBREAD CUPCAKES

Yield: 20 cupcakes

Enjoy while watching *The Nine Lives of Christmas*

2014 – Starring Brandon Routh as Zachary Stone and Kimberly Sustad as Marilee White , plus Jennifer Cheon as Sarah

Whether Marilee likes it or not, love waits for no veterinarian. (Or veterinary student.) Sarah finds her three Happy Cupcakes (matches) on dating site Just Desserts, but she has her sights set on an even more tempting treat: a handsome animal-friendly firefighter. Who can blame her?

Gingerbread Cupcakes

1½	cups all-purpose flour
2	tablespoons ground ginger
2	teaspoons ground cinnamon
¼	teaspoon ground nutmeg
¼	teaspoon ground cloves
1½	cups unsalted butter
1	cup granulated sugar
½	cup brown sugar
3	tablespoons molasses
4	large eggs, room temperature
1½	teaspoons vanilla

Cream Cheese Frosting

4	ounces cream cheese, softened
1	tablespoon ground cinnamon
½	teaspoon pure vanilla extract
2–4	tablespoons heavy cream
4	cups powdered sugar

"You've got an entire family of people in there who love you. You actually are that gingerbread family, you know that? Do you even know how special that is?"

—Isobel Gray, *Christmas List*

For the cupcakes:

1. Preheat the oven to 350°F and prepare two muffin tins with cupcake liners. In a small bowl, whisk together the flour, ginger, cinnamon, nutmeg, and cloves and set the mixture aside.

2. Add the butter and sugars to a large bowl, and use an electric mixer on low to cream them together. Mix in the molasses, then beat in the eggs one at a time until everything is well combined. Stir in the vanilla, then gradually mix in the flour mixture until well combined.

3. Fill 20 cupcake liners ¾ full with batter. Bake the cupcakes for about 25 minutes or until a toothpick inserted in the centers comes out clean. Let the cupcakes stay in the muffin tins for about 10 minutes before moving them to wire racks to cool completely.

For the frosting:

1. Using an electric mixer on medium, beat the cream cheese until it becomes fluffy, about 2 minutes. Mix in the cinnamon, vanilla, and 2 tablespoons of heavy cream until smooth.

2. Gradually mix in the powdered sugar, adding heavy cream as needed to thin out the frosting. Spread the frosting on completely cooled cupcakes and store them in an airtight container.

ELVIS'S FAVORITE CUPCAKES

⸺ Yield: 12–18 cupcakes ⸺
Enjoy while watching *Christmas at Graceland*

2018 – Starring Wes Brown as Clay and Kellie Pickler as Laurel

You can't enjoy a tribute to Elvis and the music he created without also enjoying one of his favorite food combinations: peanut butter and bananas. Just keep these creamy frosted cupcakes away from his white sofas if you're going to step over the velvet ropes.

⸺

Banana Cupcakes

1½	cups all-purpose flour
2	teaspoons baking powder
½	teaspoon baking soda
¼	teaspoon kosher salt
1	dash ground cinnamon
1	dash ground nutmeg
3	large eggs, separated
½	cup unsalted butter, softened
½	cup brown sugar
¼	cup granulated sugar
½	teaspoon pure vanilla extract
3	very ripe bananas, mashed
½	cup semisweet chocolate chips (optional)

Peanut Butter Cream Cheese Frosting

4	tablespoons unsalted butter, room temperature
4	ounces cream cheese, softened
¾	cup peanut butter
1	tablespoon honey
¼	teaspoon ground cinnamon
1	teaspoon pure vanilla extract
1–3	tablespoons heavy cream
¾	cup sifted powdered sugar

For the cupcakes:

1. Preheat the oven to 350°F and prepare two muffin tins with cupcake liners. In a small bowl, whisk together the flour, baking powder, baking soda, salt, cinnamon, and nutmeg.

2. Add the egg whites to a large bowl, and use an electric mixer on medium to whip them until stiff peaks form. Set this aside in a small dish.

3. In the same bowl, cream together the butter and sugars. Mix in the egg yolks, vanilla, and mashed bananas until well combined, then stir in the flour mixture.

4. Slowly mix in ⅓ of the egg whites. Use a spatula to gently fold in the rest of the egg whites and the chocolate chips (optional).

5. Fill the cupcake liners ⅔ full and bake the cupcakes for 15–20 minutes or until a toothpick inserted in the centers comes out clean. Let the cupcakes cool in the pans for 3 minutes, then move them to a wire rack to cool completely.

For the frosting:

1. Add the butter to a large bowl and use an electric mixer on low to beat it until light and creamy. Mix in the softened cream cheese until well combined, then the peanut butter. Mix in the honey, cinnamon, vanilla, and 2 tablespoons of the heavy cream until well combined.

2. Beat in half of the powdered sugar, then the other half. Mix in the last tablespoon of heavy cream to thin out the frosting, if necessary. Using the electric mixer on medium, beat the frosting until it's light and fluffy, about 2–3 minutes. Spread the frosting on completely cooled cupcakes and store them in an airtight container.

GRETCHEN'S EGGNOG ICE CREAM

Serves 8

Enjoy while watching *Christmas Land*

2015 — Starring Nikki Deloach as Jules and Luke Macfarlane as Tucker, plus Chonda Pierce as Gretchen

Gretchen is all too ready to reopen the ice creamery when she hears that Jules is going to keep Christmas Land going. Soon enough, she's filled the counter with "every flavor known to man"— including eggnog, of course! With just a few simple ingredients and an ice cream maker, you can bring a little Christmas Land home.

2	cups nonalcoholic eggnog
1	cup half-and-half
½	cup granulated sugar
1	teaspoon pure vanilla extract
½	teaspoon freshly grated nutmeg

1. In a large bowl, whisk together all of the ingredients until the sugar dissolves. Pour the mixture into your ice cream maker and follow the manufacturer's directions.

Note: You can enjoy the ice cream soft or let it freeze for 4 hours or more before serving.

DOUBLE MINT-CHOCOLATE CHIP ICE CREAM

Serves 8

Enjoy while watching *Switched for Christmas*

2017 – Starring Candace Cameron Bure as Kate Lockhart and Chris Dixon,
Eion Bailey as Tom Kinder, and Mark Deklin as Greg Turner

Everyone has a pint of their favorite ice cream tucked away in the freezer for emergencies, right? The go-to flavor for twins Kate and Chris is mint-chocolate chip. If you know how to make your own, you'll never be without it when you need it (although you might have to hide it from your kids behind the chicken stock).

2	cups 2% milk
2	cups heavy cream
1	cup granulated sugar
½	teaspoon kosher salt
1	teaspoon pure vanilla extract
1	teaspoon peppermint extract
3	drops green food coloring
1	cup miniature semisweet chocolate chips

1. In a large bowl, combine the milk, cream, sugar, salt, vanilla, and peppermint. Stir until the sugar dissolves, then add the food coloring until the ice cream is the shade of green you like.

2. Add the mixture to an ice cream maker and follow the manufacturer's directions. About 10 minutes into the freezing time, stir in the chocolate chips. Once the ice cream thickens, about 30 minutes, spoon it into a freezer-safe container and freeze it for another 2 hours.

CAT PAW ICE CREAM SANDWICHES

Serves 4–5

Enjoy while watching *The Nine Lives of Christmas*

2014 – Starring Brandon Routh as Zachary Stone and Kimberly Sustad as Marilee White

Marilee and Mr. Brown Eyes know that cats are much more than pets—they're furry family members, friends, roommates, and even confidants. These adorable ice cream sandwiches are a tribute to their favorite felines: Queenie and Ambrose.

1	cup unsalted butter, softened
1	cup granulated sugar
2	large eggs, room temperature
2	teaspoons pure vanilla extract
3	cups all-purpose flour
½	teaspoon baking powder
½	teaspoon kosher salt
	Pink candy melts, melted
2	pints vanilla ice cream

1. Add the butter and sugar to a large bowl, and use an electric mixer on medium to cream them together. Beat in the eggs one at a time, then mix in the vanilla extract.

2. In another large bowl, whisk together the flour, baking powder, and salt. Beat the dry mixture into the wet mixture until well combined. Divide the dough in half, wrap it tightly in plastic wrap, and refrigerate it until it firms up, at least 20 minutes.

3. Create your cat paws: For each paw, roll a ball of dough for the foot pad (about 1½ inches in diameter) and three smaller balls of dough for the toes (about 1 inch each). Arrange your paw on a parchment-lined baking sheet so that the toes and foot pad touch. Repeat with the remaining dough to create an even number of paws.

"You can listen to your mind,
but you have to follow your heart."

—Maggie Brunell, *Christmas Under Wraps*

4. Move the baking sheet to the refrigerator for 10–15 minutes before baking. Preheat the oven to 350°F, and bake the cookies for 9–11 minutes until the edges are golden brown.

5. While the cookies are still warm, use the back of two measuring spoons (one larger than the other) to create round indentations in the foot pads and toes. Let the cookies cool completely.

6. Lay the pints of ice cream on their sides and use a serrated knife to cut through the container and create ½-inch disks. Place the disks on a parchment-lined baking sheet and remove the pieces of container.

7. Use a circular cookie cutter roughly the same size as your cookies to cut out circles of ice cream from your slices. Finally, sit the cookie cutter on the baking sheet and fill it with the remnants of the ice cream discs to create another ½-inch slice. Move the baking sheet to the freezer for at least 30 minutes.

8. While the ice cream is re-freezing, fill the indentations you made in your pawprints with the melted pink candy to create the foot pad and toe beans. Let the chocolate set completely, then move the cookies to the freezer to chill until you're ready to assemble them.

9. To assemble the sandwiches, place the ice cream discs between two cookies and cut away any ice cream that sticks out. Freeze the ice cream sandwiches for 30 minutes before serving them to avoid a mess.

CARLINGSON CHRISTMAS KRINGLES

Serves 18

Enjoy while watching *Christmas in Love*

2018 – Starring Brooke D'Orsay as Ellie Hartman and Daniel Lissing as Nick Carlingson

Every Carlingson Christmas Kringle is unique and made with love, just like yours will be. These pastries may not keep a whole town afloat on their own, but they could certainly fill your coworkers (or even your undercover boss) with the Christmas spirit.

Dough

1	cup unsalted butter
2	cups sifted all-purpose flour
1	cup sour cream

Filling

¼	cup unsalted butter, softened
2	cups brown sugar
1½	cups chopped English walnuts
	More chopped walnuts, for topping

Icing

1	cup powdered sugar
2	tablespoons water

1. In a large bowl, cut the butter into the flour until crumbly. Add the sour cream and stir until the dough is well combined and sticky. Roll the dough into a ball, cover it tightly, and refrigerate it overnight.

2. Preheat the oven to 375°F and line a baking sheet with parchment paper. In a small bowl, combine the softened butter, brown sugar, and walnuts to create the filling and set it aside.

3. Take the dough out of the refrigerator and divide it into 2 equal parts. Return one half to the refrigerator and roll the other half out on a heavily floured surface to create a roughly 12 x 17-inch rectangle.

4. Using a sharp knife, create 4-inch-long, ½-inch-wide cuts diagonally along the long sides of the rectangle toward the center of the pastry. Spread ½ of the filling over the uncut center of the pastry, then crisscross the cut pieces over it in a braid-like pattern. Sprinkle additional walnuts over the top of the finished pastry.

5. Repeat steps 3 and 4 with the refrigerated portion of the dough. Arrange both pastries on the lined baking sheet and bake them for about 30 minutes until golden brown.

6. Combine the powdered sugar and the water to create the icing and drizzle it over the warm Carlingson Christmas Kringles before serving them.

LIZZIE'S CHOCOLATE YULE LOG

Serves 8

Enjoy while watching *Coming Home for Christmas*

2017 – Starring Danica McKellar as Lizzie Richfield and Neal Bledsoe as Robert Marley

Just like Lizzie Richfield herself, her favorite dessert has a way of bringing people together. This rich, chocolatey cake is one Christmas tradition that everyone can agree on, even when they can't agree on anything else. Rolling the log can be a bit tricky, so make sure you channel Danica McKellar's indomitable spirit before tackling it! Finish it off with cranberries, sprigs of rosemary, or whatever other woodsy Christmas decorations you like.

Chocolate Cake

Cooking spray

½ cup all-purpose flour

¼ cup unsweetened cocoa powder

¼ teaspoon kosher salt

6 large eggs, separated

¾ cup granulated sugar, divided

Powdered sugar, for dusting

Vanilla Filling

1 cup heavy cream

½ cup powdered sugar

1 teaspoon pure vanilla extract

Pinch kosher salt

Chocolate Buttercream Frosting

½ cup unsalted butter, softened

2 cups powdered sugar, plus more for dusting

¼ cup cocoa powder

½ teaspoon pure vanilla extract

2 tablespoons heavy cream

Pinch kosher salt

For the cake:

1. Preheat the oven to 350°F. Line a jelly roll pan or 15 x 10 x 1-inch baking sheet with parchment paper and grease the paper with cooking spray.

2. In a medium bowl, combine the flour, cocoa powder, and salt.

3. In a large bowl, use a whisk or hand mixer on low to beat the egg yolks until thick. Slowly mix in ½ cup of the sugar, then the flour mixture, until combined.

4. In another large bowl, beat the egg whites until soft peaks form. Slowly add the remaining ¼ cup of sugar and continue to mix until stiff peaks form. Gently fold half of the egg-white mixture into the egg-yolk mixture in the other bowl, then fold in the other half.

5. Pour the batter into the prepared pan to create an even layer. Bake until the top springs back when lightly pressed, about 12 minutes.

6. Dust a clean kitchen towel with powdered sugar and invert the warm cake onto the towel. Peel off the paper.

7. Starting at one short end of the cake, roll it and the towel into a tight log. Let the rolled cake cool completely while you make the filling.

For the filling:

1. Add all of the filling ingredients to a large bowl and use the hand mixer to beat the mixture until stiff peaks form. Refrigerate the filling.

2. When the cake is cool, unroll it and spread the filling evenly over it, leaving ½ inch at the edges. Without using the towel, carefully roll the cake back into a log. Place the cake seam-side down on a baking sheet and refrigerate it until it is well chilled, up to 1 hour.

For the frosting:

1. Add the butter to a large bowl and use the hand mixer to cream it.

2. Beat in the powdered sugar and cocoa powder until no lumps remain, then beat in the vanilla, heavy cream, and salt until combined.

To finish the cake:

1. Cover the cake with the Chocolate Buttercream Frosting, dragging a fork through the frosting to create the look of tree bark, and dust it lightly with powdered sugar.

CHRISTMAS WONDERLAND MILKSHAKES

Serves 2

Enjoy while watching *Christmas Wonderland*

2018 – Starring Emily Osment as Heidi Nelson and Ryan Rottman as Chris Shepherd , plus Jacob Buster and Trinity Roberts as Tom and Katie Westwood

Heidi knows that giving kids milkshakes for dinner is half the fun of being an aunt. If Tom and Katie's parents wanted them to eat their vegetables, they should have driven that rental car home a little faster. This particular milkshake, with its peppermint-vanilla flavor, is the perfect complement to Christmas.

2   cups vanilla ice cream, softened

½   cup 2% milk

½   teaspoon peppermint extract

4   chocolate sandwich cookies, crushed

1   candy cane, crushed

       Whipped cream, for serving

1. Add the ice cream, milk, peppermint extract, cookies, and crushed candy cane to a blender and blend until smooth. Divide the mixture between two glasses and top each with a healthy dollop of whipped cream.

TRADITIONAL FRUITCAKE

Serves 16

Enjoy while watching *Christmas Connection*

2017 – Starring Brooke Burns as Sydney and Tom Everett Scott as Jonathan

Whether you enjoy your fruitcake in Finland or at a complete stranger's family dinner, you'll find this traditional treat is a Christmastime staple for a reason. Whip up a few of these at the start of the season, and you'll never have to show up empty handed (or spend a week's pay at a local Christmas market).

	Nonstick cooking spray
	All-purpose flour
1	cup shortening
1	cup granulated sugar
5	large eggs
4	tablespoons pure vanilla extract
3	cups all-purpose flour
3	teaspoons baking powder
1	teaspoon kosher salt
1½	cups whole red candied cherries
1½	cups whole green candied cherries
3	cups diced candied pineapple
10	ounces golden raisins
1	pound walnut halves

1. Preheat the oven to 300°F and lightly spray and flour a 10-inch tube pan. In a large bowl, use an electric mixer to cream together the shortening and sugar until it becomes light and fluffy. Beat in the eggs and vanilla.

2. In another large bowl, combine the flour, baking powder, and salt. Add this to the wet mixture and stir until well combined, then stir in the fruit and nuts to coat.

3. Bake the fruitcake for about 2 hours until a toothpick inserted into the center comes out clean. Let the cake cool in the pan for 10 minutes before removing it and placing it on a wire rack to cool completely. Once cool, wrap the cake tightly and store it in a cool place.

CHRISTMAS ANGEL FOOD CAKE

Serves 12

Enjoy while watching *Mrs. Miracle*

2009 – Starring James Van Der Beek as Seth Webster, Erin Karpluk as Reba Maxwell,
and Doris Roberts as Mrs. Merkle

Any Christmas angel who comes with baked goods is a welcome one, and single father Seth seems duly impressed. When one of his boys asks if angels eat cake, he replies, "When it tastes like this, they do." Imagine if he had tried this extra-festive take on the classic, complete with red swirls and peppermint candies.

Cake

1   [16-ounce] box angel food cake mix

1¼   cups cold water

½   teaspoon red food coloring

1   teaspoon peppermint extract

Icing

¾   cup powdered sugar

1–2 tablespoons 2% milk

½   cup finely crushed soft
     peppermint candies

"Do angels eat cake?"
"When it tastes like this, they do!"

—Judd and Seth Webster, *Mrs. Miracle*

1. Move the oven rack to the lowest position before preheating the oven to 350°F. Add the cake mix and water to a large glass or metal bowl, and use an electric mixer on low to beat them together for 30 seconds. Increase the speed to medium and mix for 1 minute more.

2. Pour 3 cups of the batter into an ungreased 10-inch angel food cake pan. Add ¾ cup of the batter to a small bowl and stir in the food coloring and peppermint extract until well blended. Carefully spoon the red batter over the white batter in the cake pan, then carefully spoon the rest of the white batter over the red. Use a knife to swirl the batter and create a ribbon of red.

3. Bake the cake for 40 minutes or until it springs back when touched. Turn the cake upside down so that the center rests on a heat-safe object and the cake hovers above the counter. After 2 hours, turn the pan right-side up and use a knife or long metal spatula to loosen the cake. Top the pan with an upside-down serving plate, then turn everything over and pull off the pan so that the cake rests on the plate.

4. Combine the powdered sugar and 1 tablespoon of the milk in a small bowl. Add more milk if you want thinner icing. Drizzle the icing over the cake and top it with the crushed peppermint candies.

GINGERBREAD HOUSE DOUGH

Serves 4–6
Enjoy while watching *Christmas List*

2016 – Starring Alicia Witt as Isobel Gray and Gabriel Hogan as Jamie Houghton

Crafting your very own gingerbread house may have been on your Christmas to-do list since you were little, but that doesn't mean you have to (or should) make one from scratch. If you're up to the challenge and have fresh batteries in your smoke detectors, this dough recipe will help you get started.

3	cups all-purpose flour
¼	teaspoon baking soda
2	teaspoons ground ginger
2	teaspoons ground cinnamon
½	teaspoon ground allspice
¼	teaspoon kosher salt
6	tablespoons unsalted butter, softened
¾	cup packed brown sugar
1	large egg, room temperature
½	cup dark molasses
2	tablespoons water
	Royal Icing (see page 90)
	Decorating icing
	Assorted candies

1. In a large bowl, whisk together the flour, baking soda, ginger, cinnamon, allspice, and salt. Set this aside.

2. Add the butter and brown sugar to another large bowl, and use an electric mixer on medium to cream them together. Increase the speed to high and beat in the egg, molasses, and water, frequently scraping the bottom and sides.

3. Slowly add the dry mixture to the wet mixture, mixing them on low speed until well combined.

4. Divide the dough in half, flatten each half into a disc about 4–5 inches in diameter, and tightly wrap them both in plastic wrap. Let the dough chill in the refrigerator for at least 2 hours or up to 3 days.

5. Preheat the oven to 350°F and line two baking sheets with parchment paper. Remove the dough from the refrigerator and roll it out between two pieces of parchment paper until it's about ¼ inch thick.

6. Peel off the top piece of parchment paper and cut out your shapes, re-rolling the dough as necessary. Transfer the pieces to the baking sheets and bake them for 18–20 minutes or until the edges are lightly browned. Let the gingerbread pieces cool completely on a flat surface before assembling your house.

Note: You can download simple templates online or just go with a freehand design. If you get this far, you've done a lot better than Isobel!

7. Use Royal Icing to "glue" the pieces of the house together, holding things in place for a few minutes until the icing sets. Let the sides set completely before adding the roof.

8. Allow the icing to set completely, at least 4 hours but preferably overnight, before decorating with more icing and whatever candies you like.

CHRISTMAS EVE PLUM PUDDING

Serves 8

Enjoy while watching *Let It Snow*

2013 – Starring Candace Cameron Bure as Stephanie Beck and Jesse Hutch as Brady Lewis

If you're craving an old-fashioned Christmas, the only place to be is Snow Valley. Karla's mission to make the lodge feel like home for all of its visitors includes serving up traditional Christmas dishes from around the world. And it wouldn't be Christmas Eve at Snow Valley without English plum pudding!

Note: You'll need a few extras for this recipe, such as a pudding mold and a large stockpot with a rack.

Pudding

1	cup light molasses
¾	cup unsalted butter, melted
½	cup warm 2% milk
2	large eggs, beaten
1	cup all-purpose flour, plus more for tossing fruit
1	teaspoon baking soda
1	teaspoon kosher salt
1	teaspoon ground cinnamon
½	teaspoon ground cloves
1	pint candied mixed fruit
1	cup raisins
1½	ounces brandy
	Holly sprig, for garnish

Hard Sauce

¼	pound unsalted butter
1	cup granulated sugar
1	pinch kosher salt
1	teaspoon pure vanilla extract
1	ounce brandy or rum

1. In a large bowl, combine the molasses, butter, milk, and eggs. In another large bowl, combine the flour, baking soda, salt, cinnamon, and cloves. Slowly incorporate the dry mixture into the wet mixture.

2. Toss the candied fruit and raisins lightly in flour before stirring them and the brandy into the batter. Pour the pudding into a prepared pudding mold, and place the mold on the rack in your stockpot.

3. Add water until it reaches halfway up the sides of the mold. Bring the water to a gentle boil, cover the pot, and let the pudding steam for 2 hours, adding more water as needed.

4. Remove the pudding from the pot and let it rest for 5 minutes before turning it out. Meanwhile, beat together all of the Hard Sauce ingredients in a small bowl until the mixture is smooth and creamy. Serve the pudding warm with the sauce.

RISGRYNSGRÖT (CHRISTMAS RICE PORRIDGE)

Serves 5–6

*Enjoy while watching **Christmas Getaway***

2017 – Starring Bridget Regan as Emory Blake and Travis Van Winkle as Scott Hays

As travel writer Emory Blake explains, hiding an almond in Risgrynsgröt is a Swedish tradition—whoever finds it is destined to walk down the aisle. But be warned: this seemingly harmless Christmas tradition can get risky fast when the couples enjoying the porridge aren't on the same page. If you want to keep the peace, skip the almond and just enjoy the porridge.

1½   cups water

1   tablespoon unsalted butter

½   teaspoon kosher salt

1   cup jasmine rice, rinsed and drained

4½   cups 2% milk

Unsalted butter, to taste

Cinnamon-sugar, to taste

1. Add the water, butter, and salt to a medium saucepan and bring it to a boil over high heat. Stir in the rice and reduce the heat to low, continuing to stir until the boil becomes a simmer.

2. Cover the pot and let it continue to simmer for 10–15 minutes, until the rice absorbs most of the water. Uncover the pot and stir in the milk, then bring the mixture to a boil, stirring constantly, before reducing the heat to low again.

3. Once the rice comes to a simmer, cover the pot and allow it to cook, untouched, for 45 minutes. Serve the rice warm and topped with butter and cinnamon-sugar, to taste.

Note: To observe the tradition, stir in one unbleached almond before dividing the rice among bowls. Whoever finds the almond is the next to be married.

FAST FUDGE WREATH

Serves 32

Enjoy while watching **Mingle All the Way**

2018 – Starring Jen Lilley as Molly Hoffman and Brant Daugherty as Jeff Scanlon

You're a busy professional—you don't have time for elaborate desserts! This fudge takes almost no time to prepare but tastes decadent enough to impress even the most disapproving mothers. (And a little chocolate never hurts when you're stressing about getting your fledgling company off the ground.)

1	(12-ounce) bag semisweet chocolate chips
9	ounces butterscotch chips
1	(14-ounce) can sweetened condensed milk
1	teaspoon pure vanilla extract
1	(8-ounce) can walnut halves
½	cup currants
	Butter, for greasing pan
	Red and green candied cherries, for serving (optional)

1. Add the chocolate chips, butterscotch chips, and condensed milk (save the can) to a heavy pot over low heat, and stir until the chips have melted and everything is well combined and smooth. Stir in the vanilla and remove the pot from the heat, then stir in the nuts and currants.

2. Grease an 8-inch round cake pan with butter. Wrap the condensed-milk can with plastic wrap and set it in the middle of the cake pan. Spoon the fudge around the can to create your fudge wreath, then immediately decorate it with the red and green cherries (it will set quickly).

   Note: If not eating it right away, cover the fudge with plastic wrap and store it in the refrigerator.

CAROL'S HOT APPLE DUMPLINGS

Serves 8

Enjoy while watching *Christmas in Evergreen: Letters to Santa*

2018 – Starring Jill Wagner as Lisa and Mark Deklin as Kevin , plus Barbara Niven as Carol

Chris Kringle Kitchen owner Carol knows that a sugary treat can help focus the mind when you're trying to solve a couple of Christmas mysteries. Of course, these Hot Apple Dumplings are also just a great way to celebrate friends and family coming together at the holidays.

Dumplings

3	cups all-purpose flour
1	teaspoon kosher salt
1	cup shortening
1/3	cup cold water
8	medium tart apples, peeled and cored
8	teaspoons unsalted butter
9	teaspoons cinnamon-sugar, divided

Sauce

1½	cups packed brown sugar
1	cup water
½	cup unsalted butter, cubed

1. Combine the flour and salt in a large bowl, then cut in the shortening until the mixture is crumbly. Slowly stir in the water until a ball of dough forms. Divide the dough into 8 pieces, then cover it and move it to the refrigerator for at least 30 minutes.

2. Once the dough is easier to handle, preheat the oven to 350°F. Roll each piece of dough out between two pieces of parchment paper to create 7-inch squares. Place an apple in the middle of each square, and then place 1 teaspoon of butter and 1 teaspoon of cinnamon-sugar in the center of each apple.

3. Bring up the corners of the square to the center, pinching them to create a seal. (You can wet the corners with a bit of water to help them stay put.) Add the dumplings to a greased 13 x 9-inch baking dish and sprinkle them with the remaining cinnamon-sugar.

4. Add the sauce ingredients to a large saucepan and bring them just to a boil, stirring until everything is blended. Pour the sauce over the apples before putting them in the oven. Bake the dumplings for 50–55 minutes, basting occasionally with the sauce, until the apples are tender and the pastry is golden brown.

PAULINE'S CHERRY PIE

Serves 8–10

Enjoy while watching *Christmas in Homestead*

2016 – Starring Taylor Cole as Jessica McEllis and Michael Rady as Matt Larson,
plus Katrina Norman as Zoe Larson and Rhoda Griffis as Pauline

Not only can Pauline make a mean red velvet cupcake (yes, they have red velvet in Iowa, Jessica), she also makes pies good enough for siblings to argue over. If you don't have a Pauline of your own, you'll have to step up to the oven yourself. But this yummy recipe makes it easy to bake a cherry pie worthy of a small-town Christmas.

4	cups fresh or frozen tart cherries
1–1½	cups granulated sugar
4	tablespoons cornstarch
⅛	tablespoon almond extract (optional)
1	(14.1-ounce) package refrigerated pie crusts, softened
1½	tablespoons unsalted butter
1	tablespoon granulated sugar

"What's better than Christmas in Homestead? Look at it. It's perfect."

—Sophie Larson, *Christmas in Homestead*

1. Add the cherries to a medium saucepan over medium heat, cover, and cook until the cherry juice has reduced considerably, about 4–5 minutes. Remove the cherries from the heat.

2. In a small bowl, combine the sugar and cornstarch. Stir this into the hot cherries, followed by the almond extract (optional). Return the pan to the stove and continue cooking over low heat, stirring frequently, until the sauce thickens. Remove the pan from the heat and let the cherry filling cool.

   Note: You can thin the filling by adding water or thicken it by adding cornstarch, both a little at a time until you reach the desired consistency.

3. Preheat the oven to 375°F. Line a 9-inch pie plate with one of the pie crusts and fill it with the cooled cherry filling. Dot the filling with butter. Moisten the edge of the crust with a bit of water, then place the other crust on top and pinch the edges together. Sprinkle the top crust with sugar and cut a slit in the center to let the steam escape.

4. Bake the pie for about 50 minutes until the crust is golden brown. If the crust begins to get too dark, you can loosely cover it with foil for the remaining time. Let the pie cool on a wire rack before serving it.

CHOCOLATE CHESTNUT PIE

Serves 8–10

Enjoy while watching *Pride, Prejudice, and Mistletoe*

2018 – Starring Lacey Chabert as Darcy Fitzwilliam and Brendan Penny as Luke Bennett

Darcy and Luke may butt heads at first, but the way to this woman's heart includes turning her favorite Christmas tradition into a chocolatey dessert. This pie packs in all the magic of a night in the square with roasted chestnuts and wandering carolers.

Crust

24	chocolate wafer cookies, crumbled
¼	cup toasted blanched hazelnuts
1	tablespoon granulated sugar
4	tablespoons unsalted butter

Mousse & Ganache

1	cup bittersweet chocolate, finely chopped and divided
1	cup + 2 tablespoons heavy cream, divided
1	(500-gram) can sweetened chestnut puree with vanilla, divided
1	pinch kosher salt
½	teaspoon unflavored gelatin
1	tablespoon cold water

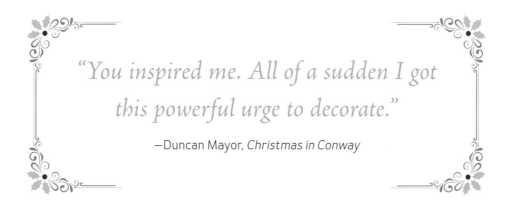

"You inspired me. All of a sudden I got this powerful urge to decorate."

—Duncan Mayor, *Christmas in Conway*

1. Preheat the oven to 350°F. Add the cookie crumbs, hazelnuts, and sugar to a food processor and pulse until fine crumbs form. Add the butter and process it until everything is well combined.

2. Press the crumbs evenly over the bottom and sides of a 9-inch glass pie plate to create the crust, then bake it for 8 minutes or until it's set. Use a flat-bottomed glass to gently tamp down the crust, then let it cool.

3. Add ⅔ cup of the chocolate to a large bowl, and place ⅓ cup of the chocolate in a separate, small bowl. Heat the cream in a large saucepan over low heat until bubbles appear around the edges. Stir 2 tablespoons of the hot cream into the small bowl of chocolate to melt it, then stir in 2 tablespoons of the chestnut puree. Set this ganache aside.

4. Pour the remaining cream into the large bowl of chocolate to melt it, then whisk in ⅔ cup of the chestnut puree plus the salt. Refrigerate this mousse mixture until it's very cold, about 2 hours. Once the mousse is cold, use an electric mixer on medium to beat it until soft peaks form.

5. Add the water to a small microwaveable bowl, then sprinkle the gelatin over top and let it soften. Microwave the gelatin until it melts, about 8 seconds. Use the electric mixer on low to beat the gelatin into the mouse.

6. Stir the remaining chestnut puree (in the can), and spread it into the pie crust. Spread the mousse over top, and move the pie to the freezer to firm up.

7. Once the mousse is firm, warm the ganache in the microwave for 10 seconds and spread it over the frozen mousse. Return the pie to the freezer until just set, then refrigerate it for 10 minutes before slicing and serving it.

EGGNOG PIE WITH A CHOCOLATE SWIRL

Serves 8–10

Enjoy while watching *Pride, Prejudice, and Mistletoe*

2018 – Starring Lacey Chabert as Darcy Fitzwilliam and Brendan Penny as Luke Bennett

Including two treats inspired by Luke Bennett's extensive catering menu may seem a bit unfair to the many bakers of cozy Christmas movies, but these delicious takes on classic Christmas flavors are worth it. Darcy said it best: Luke is like "a superhero with pie." Why choose one when you can have both?

Crust

1	cup all-purpose flour
¾	cup finely chopped nuts
¼	cup packed brown sugar
1	ounce semisweet chocolate, grated
⅓	cup butter, melted

Filling

1	pouch unflavored gelatin
¼	cup cold water
½	cup granulated sugar
2	tablespoons cornstarch
2	cups dairy or canned eggnog
1½	ounces semisweet chocolate, melted
2	tablespoons rum or ½ tablespoon rum extract
1	cup heavy whipping cream, whipped
	Grated fresh nutmeg (optional)

1. Preheat the oven to 350°F. Add the flour, nuts, sugar, and chocolate to a large bowl, then stir in the melted butter until well combined. Press this mixture into the bottom and sides of a 9-inch pie plate to form the crust. Bake the crust for 10 minutes, then let it cool on a wire rack.

2. Combine the gelatin and water in a small bowl. Add the granulated sugar and cornstarch to a large saucepan over medium heat. Stir in the eggnog, cooking and stirring until the mixture thickens and bubbles. Continue cooking and stirring for 2 minutes more, then stir in the gelatin mixture until it dissolves.

3. Divide the filling into two bowls. In one, stir in the melted chocolate. In the other, stir in the rum or rum extract. Cover both bowls with plastic wrap and move them to the refrigerator to cool for 2 hours.

4. Use a spatula to fold the whipped cream into the rum-flavored filling, then spread this mixture into the pie crust. Spread the chocolate filling over top, then use a knife to swirl and marble the two. Sprinkle nutmeg lightly over the top, if desired, then chill the pie for at least 4 hours or up to 24 hours before slicing and serving it.

BONUS:
RECIPES FOR FURRY FAMILY MEMBERS

⊱ ● ⊰

HAPPY'S HOLIDAY DOG BISCUITS

Yield: 20 treats

Give this treat while watching *A Happy & Friends Yule Log*

In addition to advocating for love and Christmas joy, cozy Christmas movies encourage viewers to adopt a furry family member from their local rescues. Happy the Dog is one such example. Between spending Christmas in front of the fire, appearing in Christmas movies (like *Switched for Christmas*), and touring the country, Happy could probably use a few of these "gingerbread men" as a pick-me-up!

1¼ cups water

¼ cup olive oil

½ cup molasses

2 tablespoons honey

3 cups organic whole wheat flour

½ teaspoon ground cinnamon

½ teaspoon ground cloves

1 tablespoon finely chopped fresh ginger

1. In a large bowl, combine the water, olive oil, molasses, and honey. In another large bowl, combine the flour, cinnamon, cloves, and ginger.

2. Stir the dry mixture into the wet mixture until well combined. Divide the dough in half, wrap each piece tightly in plastic wrap, and refrigerate them both for at least 4 hours.

3. Preheat the oven to 350°F. Remove the dough from the refrigerator and roll it out until it's ¼ inch thick. Use a cookie cutter (gingerbread man, if you have it) to cut out the biscuits, re-rolling the dough as necessary to use it up. Place the biscuits on a baking sheet and bake them for 10–15 minutes.

Note: Allow the biscuits to cool completely before giving them to any lucky pooches, and store them in an airtight container.

CHRISTMAS COOKIES FOR KITTY

Yield: 12 treats

Give this treat while watching *A Happy & Friends Yule Log*

Not long after Happy the Dog came Happy the Cat. Now they spend every Christmas together in front of the fireplace, as well as touring the country to advocate for homeless animals. This holiday season, give the felines in your life the gift of irresistible "Christmas cookies" as a thank-you for all the love they give you.

1   cup tuna

2   cups flour

1   egg

4   teaspoons dried catnip

½   cup 2% milk

1. Preheat the oven to 350°F and line a baking sheet with parchment paper. Drain the can of tuna completely, then combine all of the ingredients in a large bowl.

2. Drop the cookies by the tablespoon onto the prepared baking sheet and bake them for 8–10 minutes until firm (they won't brown). Let them cool completely before serving them to your kitty.

Note: This recipe makes large cookies, but you can break them apart and give them to your cat in bits. Store the cookies in an airtight container in the refrigerator. (You probably shouldn't exceed one cookie per cat per day.)

INDEX

CONVERSION CHARTS

METRIC AND IMPERIAL CONVERSIONS

(These conversions are rounded for convenience)

Ingredient	Cups/Tablespoons/Teaspoons	Ounces	Grams/Milliliters
Butter	1 cup/ 16 tablespoons/ 2 sticks	8 ounces	230 grams
Cheese, shredded	1 cup	4 ounces	110 grams
Cream cheese	1 tablespoon	0.5 ounce	14.5 grams
Cornstarch	1 tablespoon	0.3 ounce	8 grams
Flour, all-purpose	1 cup/1 tablespoon	4.5 ounces/0.3 ounce	125 grams/8 grams
Flour, whole wheat	1 cup	4 ounces	120 grams
Fruit, dried	1 cup	4 ounces	120 grams
Fruits or veggies, chopped	1 cup	5 to 7 ounces	145 to 200 grams
Fruits or veggies, pureed	1 cup	8.5 ounces	245 grams
Honey, maple syrup, or corn syrup	1 tablespoon	0.75 ounce	20 grams
Liquids: cream, milk, water, or juice	1 cup	8 fluid ounces	240 milliliters
Oats	1 cup	5.5 ounces	150 grams
Salt	1 teaspoon	0.2 ounce	6 grams
Spices: cinnamon, cloves, ginger, or nutmeg (ground)	1 teaspoon	0.2 ounce	5 milliliters
Sugar, brown, firmly packed	1 cup	7 ounces	200 grams
Sugar, white	1 cup/1 tablespoon	7 ounces/0.5 ounce	200 grams/12.5 grams
Vanilla extract	1 teaspoon	0.2 ounce	4 grams

OVEN TEMPERATURES

Fahrenheit	Celsius	Gas Mark
225°	110°	$1/4$
250°	120°	$1/2$
275°	140°	1
300°	150°	2
325°	160°	3
350°	180°	4
375°	190°	5
400°	200°	6
425°	220°	7
450°	230°	8